Writing for the Educational Market: Informational Books for Kids

by Laura Purdie Salas

A Children's Writer Insider Guide from Mentors for Rent™

Writing Children's Nonfiction Books for the Educational Market

Printed in the United States of America.

For information, please visit Laura Purdie Salas' website at laurasalas.com.

by Laura Purdie Salas

Table of Contents

Welcome to Writing Children's Nonfiction Books for the Educational Market!

I'm so happy to be working with you through this workbook/course!

BEFORE YOU BEGIN

Before you even read the introduction, I would like you to **request some publishers' catalogs**. Request catalogs from at least 3 of the following publishers (or from all of them if you like). It can take a while for these to arrive, so please order them right away. That way, you'll have them in hand when you get to the catalog analysis lesson!

At each publisher's website, look for a link called "Request a Catalog." If you don't see a link, type "Catalog" into the Search box. As I write this, each of these publishers is willing to send a print catalog on request. However, some publishers over the past couple of years have made the move to .pdf catalogs only. You can download the catalog to your computer, you can print it out, etc., but they don't have a paper copy to send you. I much prefer having a hard copy to flip through, write in, highlight titles, etc., but this is probably the way of the future. Sigh.

Please note: These are NOT all of the educational publishers. But they're some of the bigger ones, ones you will hear mentioned as you start working in this niche market. We'll talk later about how to find other publishers to connect with, too.

ABDO

http://www.abdopub.com

Capstone Press

http://www.capstonepub.com

Compass Point

http://www.capstonepub.com/category/LIB_PUBLISHER_CPB

Enslow

http://www.enslow.com

Heinemann-Raintree

http://www.capstonepub.com/category/LIB_PUBLISHER_HRT

Infobase Publishing

http://www.infobasepublishing.com

McGraw-Hill

https://www.mheonline.com/

Rigby

http://rigby.hmhco.com/

INTRODUCTION

I'm so pleased to be working with you! I taught this material as an online class for several years, and those classes went really well.

A number of students have gone on to write books for the educational market, which is wonderful! Others are still working on it, and that's good, too. It takes patience and persistence and determination. If you have those qualities and good writing skills as well, then you're ready to start.

I have shifted my online teaching/mentoring in other directions, though, and I decided to create a workbook containing all the materials from my online class. My travel and deadline schedule makes it difficult for me to offer extended online classes. And there's just no perfect schedule. Work, family life, school, emergencies…all of these things give each person a unique schedule. For some people, my two-week intensive workshops worked well. For others, spreading the material out over eight weeks worked better. No matter when I offered classes or on what schedule, there were still people for whom the schedule just didn't work.

So, whether I end up offering online classes or not in the future, I've decided to put the material into a book that each person can work through at his or her own pace. I hope this works out well for you!

GOALS FOR THIS WORKBOOK

Here are my goals for each one of you. After you work your way through this workbook, you will:

- understand the difference between writing for the trade and educational markets
- know whether writing books for the educational market is a good fit for you
- understand how to approach publishers for writing assignments
- have a good start on all the components you need for your introductory packets

- have identified at least 3 publishers to approach
- have a self-imposed deadline for sending out those 3 introductory packets (if you haven't already sent some or all of them by the end of the workbook)
- feel confident about your researching and writing skills, as well as your techniques for working with an editor

I hope those goals match what you want to get out of this workbook!

HOW THIS BOOK WILL WORK

Now, here's how this will work. The book is divided into 22 chapters. Each one contains the equivalent of one online lesson. It will be full of information presented in a useful, practical, casual manner. The post might contain web addresses for you to check out some online sources. For instance, I might refer to publishers' sites, or websites that are or aren't suitable for resources, or authors' websites. Or if it's something you might not be familiar with, I might give a web address so those who don't know can learn what it is.

Each post will also contain homework. These assignments are designed to help YOU get more out of the workbook. The only person who will know if you do these assignments is you. But I strongly recommend that you do them. Many students have commented that they didn't know what the purpose of a particular exercise was until after they were done. Then as they moved on, they realized how the homework reinforced what they already knew, gave them some things to think about, and moved them one step closer to the preparation of their introductory packets (that's the material you send to educational publishers to express your interest in writing books for them).

Keep in mind that this is a book for you to WORK in. Feel free to highlight stuff, circle things you don't understand or have questions about, jot notes to yourself in the margins, or whatever!

While this book contains all the material I present, I know what students really seem to value is the personal interaction and feedback. I offer several options for you to get this IF you want it.

In every class—online or in person, there are some people with lots of questions who like to bounce ideas off people, and then there are some people who just chug along, following the directions and getting things done. It's a matter of past experience, personality, and group dynamics.

If you work through this workbook and you're all set—excellent! Go for it!

If you do want personal interaction, go to www.MentorsForRent.com. That is a mentoring service that I offer with Lisa Bullard (another children's writer who does lots of writing for the educational market). Basically, you hire us by the hour, and we consult with you in either a conference phone call or an online Skype video chat. We can critique the various components of your introductory packet, answer questions about writing for this market, help you interpret editorial communications once you have an assignment...the possibilities are limitless. But that's totally optional. I hold nothing back from this textbook!

Question: Why are there two urls listed for many online sources?

Answer: In my online class, people can click on a url, and the webpage will open. Easy peasy. But for this book, you will have to type in the url on your computer. Some of the urls are extremely long, and in each of those cases, I've created a tiny url that will take you to the same webpage. That will be easier for you to type in without error. But—I'm leaving the original, long url in there, too. The reason for that is that websites get reorganized, and urls change, even when the content is still there. So here's the drill.

Try the tiny url first. 99% of the time, it will work.

If the tiny url doesn't work, look at the long url. You will be able to tell what the overall site is, like writersdigest.com, or capstonepress.com, or whatever.

Go to that basic, overall site and search for the material. If the link was supposed to be a catalog request, for instance, then look for a link that says Request a Catalog, or something like that. If the link was supposed to lead to an article, then find the Search box and type in the keywords from the title, or type in the author's name.

So, use the tiny url. It's easier. Only use the longer url to help you track down content that is no longer at the webpage it used to be on.

HOW I GOT STARTED

OK, that's how this workbook will work. Now, I wanted to share a little bit about me and how I got into educational writing.

In October of 1999, I went to a local SCBWI (http://www.scbwi.org/) conference. Editors from two educational publishers, Capstone Press (http://www.capstonepub.com/) and Lerner (http://www.lernerbooks.com) spoke at the conference. Because I was conference volunteer (always a great idea), I got to be one editor's helper and I got a manuscript critique with the other. I ended up writing books for both companies.

I didn't go to the conference thinking, "Educational publishing: that's for me!" But I was one of those kids who liked writing reports in school. Were you? So as the editors described how they worked, I thought, "I could do this!"

I had been submitting (bad) picture book manuscripts and magazine stories for a couple of years. I had a few publications, but I really wanted to write a book. So when Jill Braithwaite (who was an editor at Lerner at that time) asked if I would be interested in writing a biography, I said, "Sure!"

Even though history is my weakest subject and a biography was by far NOT my first choice.

And thus began my history of educational publishing. As of the end of 2010, I've written about 90 nonfiction books for the educational market, and I have 10 poetry books for the educational market, too.

http://laurasalas.wordpress.com/2008/01/07/my-capstone-poetry-books/
http://tinyurl.com/7kxbjup

Poetry and verse are my first loves. If I could have a career solely as a children's poet, I would. But I enjoy doing my nonfiction work, too. It makes me feel like a "real" writer to get things published regularly and to earn my income from writing and writing-related activities. My first trade picture book, **Stampede! Poems to Celebrate the Wild Side of School** (http://www.stampedebook.com/) (Clarion, 2009) was a finalist for the Minnesota Book Award. My second trade picture book, **BookSpeak! Poems About Books** (Clarion, 2011), is out, and I have a brand new rhyming nonfiction picture book, **A Leaf Can Be**..., with Millbrook Press (2012). So my writing career is a mix of books for the trade market and the educational market (more on the difference between trade and educational books soon).

Over the years, I have taught 8th-grade English, worked for magazines, done freelance writing for newspapers and grown-up magazines, worked for the Minneapolis *Star Tribune* website (http://www.startribune.com/) as an editor for 10 years, and taught for the Institute of Children's Literature.

http://www.theinstituteofchildrensliterature.com/G2685/
http://tinyurl.com/26yldn6

I have a varied work background, to say the least, but I think my various ways of working with words have been good for me.

I've written books for Capstone, Compass Point, and Picture Window Books, which are all sister companies and part of Coughlan Companies (http://www.coughlan-companies.com/); Lerner; Steck-Vaughn (http://steckvaughn.hmhco.com/en/steckvaughn.htm); Zaner-Bloser (http://www.zaner-bloser.com/); Trillium (http://www.trilliumpublishing.com/); and others.

What else? I grew up in Florida but live in Minnesota with my husband and two daughters.

OK, this is much longer than I meant it to be. So, on to homework!

HOMEWORK

1. Jot down your thoughts on the following questions.
   - What kind of writing do you like to do?
   - Are you published?
   - What drew you to this workbook?
   - What are you hoping to get out of it?

Lesson One

The Trade Market vs. the Educational Market

Maybe you already have some publishing experience, and you might already know the difference between trade publishers and educational publishers. Or maybe, like many writers and readers, you haven't been aware of these two very different publishing processes. Understanding the difference between trade and educational publishing is key to starting your work as an educational writer. So in this lesson, I'm spelling out the differences between the two and what those differences mean to you.

OVERVIEW OF THE EDUCATIONAL MARKET

First, we'll talk about what exactly is meant by the Educational Market.

The **educational market is the group of books published mainly for school libraries to buy**. Here's a brief overview.

Ages:

K-12 - Books for very young kids, preschool ages, are often written by reading specialists or written in-house by editors. And high school students often read adult nonfiction books. So, the vast majority of educational market books are written for the 1st-9th grade market, with 4th-8th grade being the sweet spot. Still, publishers do hire freelance writers for books for kindergarteners all the way up through high school students.

Reading Level:

Standard books - These are books that have a reading level that matches the age of the audience. A book written about a state might be written at the 4th-grade level, and the main audience is 4th graders.

High/Low books - These books are written for kids who are not reading at grade level. They might be reading below grade level for many reasons: they are English language learners (ELL, formerly known as ESL), they might have learning disabilities, or they might just hate to read and don't get enough practice at it. For instance, my skateboarding book for Steck-Vaughn is for 7th- or 8th-grade students but was written at strict 2nd-grade level.

http://www.laurasalas.com/nonfiction/nfbks/thrill.html
http://tinyurl.com/29xtrne

It has a design and cover and dimensions (known as the trim size) of a book for older kids, but the language is extremely simple. That's because 7th graders wouldn't be caught dead reading a book that LOOKED like it was written at a 2nd-grade reading level. Other high/lows are not as precise, like my outdoor recreation books for Capstone books, which you can see listed under Social Studies and Recreation here.

http://www.laurasalas.com/nonfiction/bks3rdup.html
http://tinyurl.com/2dprvsa

They are written at about the 5th-grade level and are considered appropriate for about 4th- through 9th-graders.

Topics:

Standard curriculum topics - Social studies and science are very common topics. There are not as many math books published (other than textbooks, and that's not what we're talking about), and literature is not written much on assignment. So, the great majority of books are social studies and science. Books on landforms, periods of history, animals, scientific processes...every level and topic within those two subjects is covered, it seems.

Other topics - Biographies are huge for all age ranges, even down to first and second grade. Careers are a popular topic, both for career planning and also just for awareness of different jobs as "community helpers." I did a few books like this one for K-2 (kindergarten through second grade) for Picture Window Books that were considered "career books," because they dealt with jobs, identifying different workers by the shoes they wore, or the gloves or the jackets they wore.

http://www.laurasalas.com/nonfiction/nfbks/shoes.html
http://tinyurl.com/2cw3aol

Social skills themes are big, too, like self-esteem. Social issues and controversial topics, like euthanasia and divorce, are also heavily covered.

High-interest topics (high/lows) are often written strictly to get reluctant readers to read. Sometimes these titles seem like tabloid-style books, but the same rigorous research goes into them that goes into the more standard books.

http://www.amazon.com/Searching-Aliens-Black-Unexplained-Phenomena/dp/1429648163/ref=sr_1_8?s=books&ie=UTF8&qid=1323025331&sr=1-8
http://tinyurl.com/7xjtgub

Publishers simply play up the fantastic aspects in order to lure kids into reading.

Tone:

The tone of educational books has historically been very straightforward. They typically use active language, but are not overly dramatic. Clarity takes priority over "fun" writing. You can't be ambiguous. Some educational publishers use (or at least incorporate in sidebars, etc.) some fun facts and punchier writing. Over the past 10 years, educational books have changed a lot. Publishers do still publish straightforward books, but they increasingly incorporate good design, fun illustrations, and a more contemporary voice. They are books that look fun or interesting to read, whether you have to write a report on a topic or not. Most educational market books are 3rd-person, but some lend themselves to a more personal, 2nd-person point of view. Some even use humor and fun formats to appeal to kids.

Format:

More than 99% of books from educational publishers are **PUBLISHED IN SERIES**. Some publishers do a very few stand-alone titles (that's what it's called when it's one book, not a series), but this is the rare exception. Series books are very similar in format and style, differing only in content/topic (lots more on this later).

THE DIFFERENCE BETWEEN TRADE AND EDUCATIONAL PUBLISHERS

So, what's the difference between trade and educational publishers?

Here is the main, #1, most important difference between the two kinds of publishers:

For a trade publisher, a writer writes the manuscript she loves and tries to sell it.

For an educational publisher, a writer identifies publishers he would like to write for and tries to get assignments to write books.

Let's look at that more closely.

For a trade publisher, a writer writes the manuscript she loves and tries to sell it. She chooses the age range, the angle of approach, the tone, etc. She then tries to sell the manuscript to a publisher who will in turn try to sell it to bookstores, libraries, and schools.

For an educational publisher, a writer identifies publishers he would like to write for. He approaches those publishers with an introductory packet and convinces them he is a professional, competent writer. An educational publisher assigns the writer to write a certain book on a particular topic for a definite age range. The publisher provides series guidelines to the writer, and he writes the book according to what the publisher has asked for. He writes the book in a way that it will *not* stand out on its own but will fit perfectly into the series the publisher has conceived. The publisher sells the book mainly to schools, and also to public libraries.

That's the biggest difference right there. Here's a chart to help you see the other differences.

	Trade Publisher	**Educational Publisher**
Write the book...	first, and submit to publishers.	after an editor assigns you the book and provides guidelines and samples.
The book is sold...	in bookstores, public libraries, online, and in school libraries.	in school libraries, online, and in public libraries.
The book...	stands alone. Usually not part of a series.	is part of the series. It must fit into the rest of the series.
Copyright is owned...	by the writer. You sell certain rights to publish it, but you own the work itself.	by the publisher. The work belongs to the publisher, now and forever.
You are paid...	with advance and royalties. Say you get 10% royalties (very generous nowadays) on a $20 book (so that's $2 per book sold). You get a $5,000 advance. After the book sells 2,500 copies ($5,000 worth of royalties), THEN you begin to earn royalties. The more the book sells (or the less), the more (or less) you earn.	Generally with a flat fee that does not change, no matter how many copies the book does or does not sell. You may Make anywhere from $500 to $4,000 per book, and you will generally get paid very promptly.
The books...	may or may not relate to the school curriculum (though the trend is for even trade publishers to look for school tie-ins).	almost always tie in to the school curriculum.

CAN YOU WRITE FOR BOTH KINDS OF PUBLISHERS?

Many writers write for both the trade and the educational market. Sally Walker wrote *Fossil Fish Found Alive*, one of my favorite trade nonfiction [nf] books.

http://www.amazon.com/Fossil-Fish-Found-Alive-Discovering/dp/1575055368/ref=pd_bbs_sr_1?ie=UTF8&s=books&qid=1199798414&sr=1-1
http://tinyurl.com/22o6n87

She also wrote *Secrets of a Civil War Submarine*, which won the Sibert Award, *Blizzard of Glass: The Halifax Explosion of 1917*, and several other excellent trade market books. Walker is a highly skilled writer.

Sibert:

http://www.ala.org/ala/mgrps/divs/alsc/awardsgrants/bookmedia/sibertmedal/index.cfm
http://tinyurl.com/mh8rs7

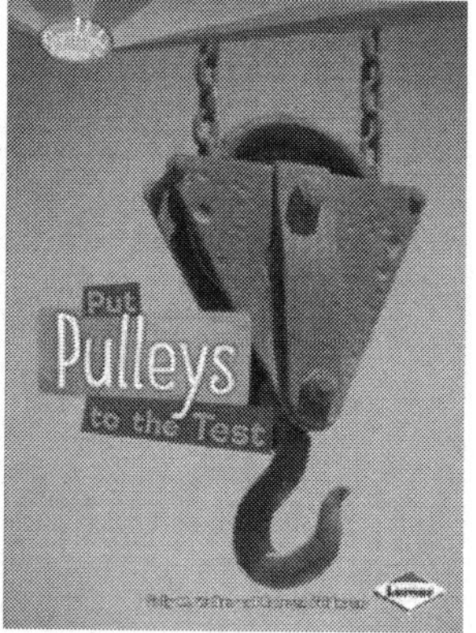

But Walker also writes for the educational market. Check out her listings at Amazon.com and you'll see many books with series titles in parentheses.

http://www.amazon.com/Sally-M.-Walker/e/B001HCX4MG/ref=sr_1_1?qid=1323026126&sr=8-1-ent
http://tinyurl.com/7jfwf8g

Most of the books listed there are published by educational publishers.

Melissa Stewart (http://www.melissa-stewart.com/) is another talented writer who writes for both trade and educational publishers.

There used to be two kinds of nonfiction writers. There were those who wrote for trade markets and those who wrote for educational markets. But the line dividing those groups has blurred, if not completely disappeared. Like Hollywood stars who do commercials overseas, some trade nonfiction writers look to educational writing to provide them with steady writing projects and steady income. You no longer have to limit yourself to one or the other.

That said, I know many nonfiction writers who fall squarely into one camp or the other. I know trade writers who can't imagine a publisher calling the shots on a writing project. And I know a number of writers who simply love educational nonfiction and the straightforward satisfaction of writing for the educational market. They write exclusively for educational publishers, and some even make a living at it. You will not grow rich writing for educational publishers. But some people who work extremely hard can support themselves doing it. Most use it as a supplementary income, however. I'll get into more detail about the money side of things later in the book.

I write for both kinds of publishers, and I have written fiction, nonfiction, and poetry for both kinds of publishers. Fiction and poetry for work-for-hire publishers is a much less common thing, but it is out there. I'll talk just a tiny bit about this later in the book, as it's definitely not the focus here! I enjoy the contrast between writing what I absolutely love and hope to sell and writing on assignment, knowing that the work will be published and I will be paid for it. There's something to be said for that!

So now that you've learned more about writing for the educational market, what do you think?

HOMEWORK

Make yourself a list of the pros and cons of writing for the educational market and the trade market. These will vary from person to person, so this is not an absolute list with right and wrong answers. It's personal to you. Some people find the idea of selling all rights to their work terrifying, while others have no problem with it. Spend 10 minutes or so thinking about writing for the educational market. What do you like about it? What do you dislike about it? Also think about whether you're interested in writing exclusively for the educational market or whether you plan to write for both educational and trade markets.

Note: You'll be analyzing catalogs soon. Hopefully, the ones you requested have started coming in. If not, don't panic. Most publishers have their catalogs online, and you can still do the exercises without a hard copy of a catalog. But if you haven't requested any catalogs yet, you probably will still want to do that. That way you can browse and analyze them later at your leisure. They're a goldmine of info!

FREQUENTLY ASKED QUESTIONS [FAQ]

1) *Are all educational publishers work-for-hire?*

About 95% of educational publishers are work-for-hire. But some aren't. Enslow, for instance, pays an advance and royalties. Sleeping Bear kind of straddles the line between a trade and an educational publisher. They pay advance and royalties. But they rarely purchase finished manuscripts. They mostly assign topics. Millbrook Press and Charlesbridge are two more publishers that kind of blur the line.

(A digression: Millbrook, in fact, decides for each book it publishes whether that book will be priced as a trade book or an educational market book. Ed market books are more expensive because they are heavy-duty bound (library-bound) to survive the handling they'll get at schools. Also, because, I assume, they can charge more to institutions than to individuals. Trade books are priced at the $15-$20 that you typically see bookstore books priced at. They decide this based on whether the book will have broad bookstore appeal or not. When I sold *A Leaf Can Be...* to Millbrook, they told me that they would decide about a year before the publication date how the book would be priced and marketed. Interesting!)

So, there *are* some publishers that publish books mainly for school libraries but pay advance and royalties. It can feel confusing at first, but just hang in there. As you learn how to research different publishers, you'll be able to find the info you need in order to approach the publishers that interest you.

2) *Would you ever pitch a series idea to an educational publisher?*

Educational publishers' series are carefully chosen with lots of curriculum consideration. So almost all of their series ideas come from in-house. But many are mostly happy to hear your idea. What I would do is, in your introductory packet (we'll get to that), in your cover letter, say that you have an idea for a social studies series on xyz topic. Would they be interested in seeing a brief proposal? Then if they say yes, you do just a one- or two-page proposal overview. At that point, they might take the ball and run with it and create the specifics in-house based on their own needs, or they might ask you for a more in-depth proposal. Or they might decline.

3) *There's another kind of book I see in schools a lot. It's what seems to have replaced the basal reader in some schools--books that they use during reading time that "look" like trade books, not like text books. Only the whole class is reading the same book and they bought it from a textbook publisher. They read a bunch of these books instead of the old book with lots of stories we read as kids. I have some reading education background, and I'd love to get into doing these sets as well, but I don't have a clue how. Are they all done in-house?*

I think what you're referring to are leveled readers. Some publishers, Zaner–Bloser and SRA McGraw–Hill, for instance, publish sets of books in different grades and reading levels. They often come in units that include both fiction and nonfiction books related to a certain theme or topic. With leveled readers, a publisher will often tell you they need a book written at the 2.3–grade level, for instance. That's second grade, third month. They will give you or refer you to tools to test your book's readability. It could be as simple as using Flesch–Kincaid tool in Word (more on that later), or it could be a much more time–consuming, very particular kind of leveling.

Also, in leveled readers, you usually only get two author's copies, and you are frequently responsible for laying out the book—figuring out which text goes on which page and adding directions for the artist/designer (these directions are call art specs). Writing leveled readers is a lot like putting together a jigsaw puzzle.

They're a kind of specialty subset of educational publishing, and a reading education background would make you a great candidate to write these. They're more complicated and time–consuming to write, but pay a bit better, too!

4) *On the link to Sally Walker's Fossil Fish Found Alive I noticed she had two books on essentially the same subject--that coelacanth fish. One was a Carolrhoda photograph book, and the other was an early reader, like a step-into-reading type book (I forget which publisher). That seems really smart, if you can double your research. I'd love to be able to do a work-for-hire book, and then pitch a similar book, but on a different reading level, or focused a little differently, to a trade publisher. Or vice versa.*

Exactly! Isn't that brilliant? Now, *some* publishers' contracts include a non–compete clause where you can't write about the same topic for the same age range (which they define VERY broadly) for a certain number of years. So that's something to think about, and I'll discuss that more when we get to contracts.

But overlapping your research is a major plus to writing for both trade and educational markets. Many historical fiction writers put their research to use in the educational market, too. Or vice versa. They start out doing educational writing and become fascinated by a topic or time period and weave it into their fiction. Cool, right?

5) *Do books written for the educational market get reviewed and win awards?*

American Library Awards (like the Newbery, Printz, Caldecott, Sibert, etc.) don't generally go to educational market titles. They are strongly, strongly tied to the trade market. Some educational market book do win awards, but they often come from the Association of Educational Publishers.

http://www.aepweb.org/awards/index.htm
http://tinyurl.com/2627zjz

But some other organizations offer awards that can go to educational publisher books, too. The National Council for Social Studies, for instance, has both trade and educational publisher books on their awards list. The 2010 list, for instance, includes *Catherine the Great: Empress of Russia,* from Franklin Watts' Wicked History series.

http://www.socialstudies.org/notable
http://tinyurl.com/74s3sse

And the National Science Teachers Association does their Outstanding Science Trade Book Awards. These lists honor "trade books," but really, they just mean not textbooks, I think.

http://www.nsta.org/publications/ostb/?lid=tnav
http://tinyurl.com/7v6clw3

Most of the books on these lists are from trade publishers, like FSG, Walker, etc. But there are a few titles there from Enslow, Benchmark, and others. So awards are a possibility.

In fact, one of my poetry books for Capstone Press was shortlisted for the Utah Readers' Choice Award, which is lots of fun.

http://www.granitemedia.org/2010/03/2011-beehive-book-award-nominees/
http://tinyurl.com/6p8h7a7

I have subscribed to *The Horn Book* for many years, and it does not review titles from educational publishers. Though I'm not sure about their *Guide* or other publications. Some journals don't review educational titles because of the journals' lead times. Books have to be available 6 months to a year ahead of time if you want them reviewed. Educational market books are produced much more quickly than trade books, and they can't fit in journals' lead times. I believe SLJ (*School Library Journal*: http://www.schoollibraryjournal.com/) does mainly trade titles. Though I do see a few books on Enslow's site that have reviews from SLJ.

Most educational market book reviews come from smaller sources: Library Media Connection (http://www.librarymediaconnection.com/), Children's Literature (http://www.clcd.com/), etc. *Booklist* sometimes reviews educational market books, too.

http://www.ala.org/ala/aboutala/offices/publishing/booklist_publications/booklist/booklist.cfm
http://tinyurl.com/pcmztp

VOYA—Voice of Youth Advocates—(http://www.voya.com/) does, too. Titles for teens seem more likely to get reviewed than titles for younger kids, in general.

So, yes, some educational market books get reviewed in journals. But most of them don't. And because educational publishers are selling to a more defined, "captive" audience—school libraries—reviews don't seem to be *quite* as sought after as they are by trade pubs.

6) *Is it hard to write about topics you're not passionate about?*

If you're a naturally curious person, then I don't think it is. For me, it's always interesting to learn about new topics. And because the turnaround time is fairly short for most educational market books, by the time I'm starting to get bored, the book is due anyway!

Also, writing about your passion can actually be a downside when writing for the educational market. I had a friend who got contracts to write about dance--her lifelong passion and former (before an injury) career. But she was too close to the topic and had a terrible time with the projects. She couldn't bear to leave stuff out and hated following what the publisher wanted to emphasize, rather than what she wanted to share.

So, while writing my *From Mealworm to Beetle* book wasn't a whoop-di-loop swirl of excitement :>) it also caused me no stress at all. Just something to consider for everyone who has certain topics/passions they want to write about. It can sometimes be a double-edged sword, since it's harder to give up control, in my opinion, on topics you care deeply about.

Lesson Two

Finding Publishers and Catalogs

I hope you did some good thinking for your list of pros and cons about writing for the educational market. Remember, you are in control. If you approach and get an offer from a publisher who does work-for-hire (WFH) assignments only, you can certainly decline. And we'll talk later about how to do research so that you find that out BEFORE you approach them, anyway! I will say that books for younger kids, K-3, say, are almost exclusively work-for-hire, so I'm not sure you'd find royalty series there in the educational market.

OK, onto this lesson's topic.

FINDING EDUCATIONAL PUBLISHERS

There are so many publishers that publish books for the educational market. The well-known ones, like the ones I suggested you obtain catalogs from, get many writers approaching them, hoping to be hired to write books. That doesn't mean you shouldn't try there. Larger publishers put out more books and need more writers.

But you should also approach smaller, lesser-known publishers. But how do you find them?

There are lots of sources for **finding publishers**. Here are a few to try:

• **Browse a school library**. Pull series books off the shelves and look them over. If they appeal to you at first glance, write down the publisher names to research. Ask the librarian or media specialist about her favorite publishers to buy from. She might have a catalog you can study, too.

• **Join NFforKids**, an email list for children's nonfiction writers. Look at people's sig lines (signature lines--the lines below their names on their emails) and see with whom they've published books.

http://groups.yahoo.com/group/NFforKids/
http://tinyurl.com/2d75bgz

• **Read *Children's Writers & Illustrators Market*** (published by Writer's Digest Books and available at most bookstores, plus online at amazon.com or bn.com or indiebound.org). The entries with an apple icon are considered educational publishers.

• Check out the **Yahoo Education Publishers Directory.**

http://dir.yahoo.com/Business_and_Economy/Shopping_and_Services/Publishers/Education/Supplementary_Materials/
http://tinyurl.com/56o9q

• If you're a teacher or librarian, **go to a conference** directed toward teachers and librarians (like your state's ALA [American Library Association] conference or your region's IRA [International Reading Association] conference). Educational publishers set up booths at these to advertise their books.

• Read the fantastic **Writing for the Education Market blog** (http://educationwriting.blogspot.com/). These are often assessment and textbook-related postings, but there have been book publishers mentioned here, too.

• Check out the listing on Evelyn B. Christensen's page, but with a caveat! **Please don't start considering all these publishers until you finish this workbook.**

http://www.evelynchristensen.com/markets.html
http://tinyurl.com/7475y2m

At this point, this list would likely confuse you. She calls them educational publishers, and they all publish nonfiction books in their line. But these are **NOT ALL** educational publishers in the traditional industry sense, as I'm defining educational publishers in this textbook. Once you finish this workbook, you'll have a good sense of how educational publishers work, and it will be easier for you to discern whether a publisher is trade or educational. That's when Evelyn's terrific listing will be useful for you!

YOU HAVE A PUBLISHER'S NAME—NOW WHAT DO YOU DO?

Once you find the name of an educational publisher and you want to learn more about it, you can do two main things: study the website and study a catalog.

Getting catalogs is easy. If you go to the company's website, there will almost always be a Request a Catalog link somewhere on the home page. Just click on the link, fill out the form, and submit it. Within a few weeks, you'll have a catalog in your hands. Please note: If you are not in the United States, some publishers will not ship a catalog to you for free. You can email their customer service and ask if you can send an envelope with postage on it. Or if you explain that you're an aspiring writer, maybe some will be kind enough to send you one, anyway!

In the form, when it asks for your school, just put "Children's writer."

Check out the introduction to this book to find the web addresses to catalog request pages for a few publishers, if you didn't already do that.

HOMEWORK

Spend some time online browsing the websites of some educational publishers. Jot down the names of 4–5 that look interesting, that publish books you might be proud to say you wrote. Request their catalog (if you didn't already). In the next chapter, we'll move on to in-depth catalog analysis. Right now, we're just browsing several and getting a sense of what's being published by educational publishers today.

FAQ

1) *What if a publisher says they don't accept submissions?*

In general, closed educational houses are a conundrum (they aren't that common, but some of the bigger ones are turning this way). Some really don't want to see anything from potential writers. Others have that policy simply because hundreds of writers are sending completed manuscripts, which they don't want or need.

Lerner is one such closed house. But I've had students contact them with intro packets. Two got responses (and one of those got an assignment shortly after that; one got a form letter saying they don't take unsolicited materials). So some of it is simply the luck of the draw—who opens your packet.

Or you could try emailing the general contact info from the website and explaining briefly that you realize they are a work-for-hire publisher, and you are a freelance writer looking for assignments within the educational market. Would they be interested in seeing an introductory packet from you?

You could also ask on email lists and boards (see the resources list at the back of the book) if anyone has published with that publisher. That person might be willing to share info and perhaps even an editor name.

No matter how you do it, if you can get an editor's name to send to (more on this in a few lessons), that helps.

There are so many more open than closed houses. For the most part, I'd recommend starting with the open ones, as most publishers are. And then when you discover a house whose books you *absolutely* love, you submit to them even if they do say closed. But, starting out, especially, your odds are certainly better with houses that do not call themselves closed.

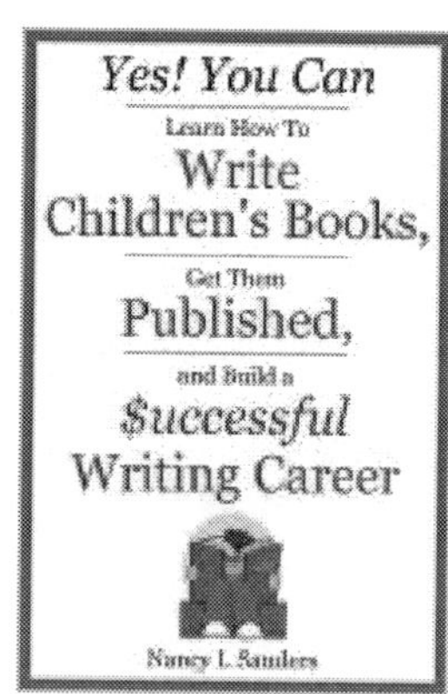

I want to share (with permission) an email from the NFforKids list. Nancy Sanders is talking about Sleeping Bear Press here, but the information applies to any of them.

Some publishers say they only work with agented submissions, so I know I can't submit to them directly since I do not have an agent at this time.

But if the publisher only says they don't take unsolicited submissions, I will consider contacting them with a short e-mail query if I really feel I have a strong potential book for their product line.

So, I just found a generic e-mail for them on their website, and sent them a short e-mail that said basically:

Dear Submission Editor:

I have studied your website and have read your alphabet books. I like your alphabet series! I noticed you don't have an alphabet book yet about African American history, yet you have one on Native American history. Would you be interested in receiving a proposal for an alphabet book about African American history?

They e-mailed me right back and said sure!

After I wrote my book for them I asked them why they have that notice on their website and they said that so many people send them random picture book manuscripts that don't even fit into their product line that they've had to post that.

I've known other authors who have approached them this same way and gotten responses, too!

Notice that I didn't write my book FIRST, but just contacted them with a topic that would fit into their product line. Then we worked on the proposal together and fine-tuned it to fit into their list. Then I wrote the book under contract. That's how I work with most of my publishers to land contracts and it seems to work.

Best,
Nancy
Nancy I. Sanders
Web site: www.nancyisanders.com
Blog: www.nancyisanders.blogspot.com

And here's more from a follow-up email she sent me:

"So, I just end up e-mailing editors of publishers I'm interested in. If they never e-mail back, I just move on and forget about them. But if they e-mail back (as many do!) then we start dialoging until a contract.

Here's the steps I follow:

1. Study a publisher's product line and find a topic that would fit into one of their series.

2. E-mail them a short query--like 5 sentences! I state I've studied their website, like their series, like a title in their series, and have an idea for a topic within that series. Then I ask them if they'd like to see a proposal for that topic, and if not I list 3 other topics that might work, too.

3. If they don't respond, I just cross them off my list.

4. If they do respond, I get the proposal ready within a month and make sure it fits exactly into their product line. I e-mail the proposal. Even if it says to snail mail the proposal, I always e-mail that editor the proposal FIRST and ask if that's okay or should I send it snail mail. I've found that if I send it snail mail, someone might not pick it up for months from the manuscript pile and it will be forgotten! But since I've already been e-mailing the editor, she usually just takes it no problem and moves it right along!

Happy writing!"

OK, so this is similar to what we'll talk about soon for our cover letters. I don't want to get into more detail now, but this is just a nice preview!

There are many approaches we can take to getting published! Generally, I don't recommend emailing as a very beginner, because it turns some editors off a lot. But, if you have a real persistent attitude and it won't bother you to not get a response, it can be a valid way to approach publishers. And if you keep it very short and sweet and make it obvious that you're professional and that you've done your homework and studied the publisher BEFORE emailing them, that helps!

Lesson Three

Open Up Those Catalogs!

Now, I know you might be a little confused or overwhelmed. There are so many publishers, and so many kinds of books, and it can all feel like too much to wrap your brain around. It's like when I was teaching myself to sew. I unfolded that enormous tissue pattern with a million pieces drawn on it and thought, "Uh oh." There was no way I could figure that all out. But I did, one tiny step at a time.

So stay with me, and we'll do this one small step at a time:>) We're going to learn about standard educational publishing here. That's our focus. Once you know how that works, you might choose to move into leveled readers, teacher materials, assessment materials (for standardized testing—see Lesson Nineteen), etc. And that's great! But we'll focus on the simplest, most basic unit of educational publishing. We're going to focus on the books of the kind put out by Capstone, Enslow, etc. These kinds of books make up more than 80% of the market, and once you know how to do them, you will know how to approach publishers for other, more specialized kinds of work. And even just looking at those kinds of publishers can be overwhelming. So I would suggest not trying to look at more than a couple of publishers per day, max. And if one doesn't appeal to you at all, add their name to a list of Publishers I Don't Really Want to Write For. There are enough publishers that you can find ones you like. Don't waste your time on ones whose books turn you off.

WHAT DO YOU LOOK FOR WHEN ANALYZING A CATALOG?

A publisher's catalog is gold for a writer. You can learn all sorts of information about the publisher simply by studying the catalog. You'll also learn information that will help you make a good impression in your introductory packet.

Here are some things to be aware of when studying a nonfiction publisher's catalog:

- What subjects are covered?
- What's the audience age range?
- Does the publisher put out Hi/Lo books, standard books, or both?
- What is the tone/feel/voice of the books, in general?
- Are there many one-author series?
- Read the excerpts given. Do some of the books have a writing style you like?
- Are there reviews from journals like *School Library Journal*? That's a good thing.
- Are any award-winning books noted? Another good thing!
- Do you find the general look of their books appealing?
- Which series interest you? Mark those pages!
- Are there any series that you would have particular expertise about?
- Which series are marked "NEW"? These might be more open to new authors.

ONE PUBLISHER'S CATALOG

OK, let's look at a couple of catalog pages together. I just want to take you through my train of thought as I browse a catalog.

Let's use Enslow's Fall 2011 catalog, which is online.

http://ecatalog.enslow.com/T13_eCatalog/
http://tinyurl.com/75x7awj

From the cover, I can tell that Enslow publishes books for preschool, elementary, middle and high school. So there could be something for everyone here!

A SERIES FOR YOUNG KIDS

First, go to page 17 (print it out if that makes it easier for you to work with). This looks like a fun new series: Far-Out and Unusual Pets. From this page, I can see that these books are aimed at 3rd to 4th graders, and that each book covers one animal. From the Each Title box, I see they're 48 pages long, and since I can see a whole spread, I see that sometimes pages are text only, some are photo only (and I'm guessing some are a mix). Each book also contains words to know, learn more (a list of books and websites for more info), and an index. As the writer, I'll probably be expected to write all of those (except, usually, the index).

I notice that all six books in this new series are by Alvin and Virginia Silverstein and Laura Silverstein Nunn. That makes me wonder if this family team is going to be the only author for the series. But not necessarily. Ed publishers usually publish 4-6 books in a series each season. So it could be that the Silversteins just did this first set. There are certainly plenty more animals that could be added to this series, which is promising. (If there were 16 books in this series, all by the Silversteins, I would consider them the series authors and wouldn't bother trying to break into the series unless it was one I couldn't live without!)

Let's look at the listing for *Hissing Cockroaches* (eeeeuwwww!). (BL, SLJ, WC) These abbreviations tell you which publications or groups reviewed this book. So Booklist, School Library Journal, and Wilson Catalog all reviewed and/or recommended this title.

978-0-7660-3685-7 is the ISBN number. It's the number libraries and bookstores use to identify and order books. As the writer, the ISBN doesn't matter to you at this point.

L4.2/P0.5 This is Accelerated Reader info. This program is used in many schools to track kids' reading. Basically, this tells you that this book is Leveled at 4.2 (4th grade) and is worth .5 Points. You don't need to know the Points, but it's helpful to know the reading level.

Now I know a fair amount about these books. And if I want to know the word count, to get a better feel for the length of books, I can go to Renaissance Learning and type in the title. This company is actually the creator of Accelerated Reader program.

http://www.renlearn.com/store/quiz_home.asp
http://tinyurl.com/y42sd4

When the title comes up and I click on it, I find that this book is 3,404 words. If this were a book for really young kids, K-1, say, it might have as few as 500 words.

A SERIES FOR OLDER KIDS

OK, let's check out a series for older kids, and one that has multiple authors. Go to page 69 (of the catalog itself, not of the pdf) and look at American Rebels.

I see this series has 11 titles going back to 2006. It's unusual for a series to be added to so sporadically, but since these are for high school students, they're obviously longer and they don't add to series of longer books with quite the same speed as they do for shorter books for younger readers. The good news is that five different authors wrote these 11 titles, so no one author has a proprietary hold on this series.

The page tells me the series is for grades 9–12. The books are typically 160 pages and have color and b&w photos. Who's responsible for finding the images? That's something I would ask if I were offered a title. Once you get to middle school and high school books, publishers usually change to black and white images. Color images of younger books are more appealing, but often books for older readers switch to b/w, since it's cheaper to publish. It's nice that these have both.

I go to Renaissance Learning again and look up the Madonna title. It's almost 25,000 words. Often, books for older readers aren't in Renaissance because (I assume) the Accelerated Reader program isn't used as much with older students.

Each book contains a glossary, a timeline, a further reading list, Internet addresses, and an index, of which I'd expect to do the first three, and hopefully not the fourth.

Finally, I noticed in the Table of Contents that the new series are clearly identified. If I wanted to approach Enslow, I would definitely check out these new series to find ones that had both more than one author and also appealed to me. I'll talk more later about where you'll mention these specific series.

One other note: Some of the things I mentioned here, about images and indices, are because of things other writers have said about Enslow. Enslow requires—or used to require––many of its writers to provide the images for the books—at the writer's expense. It's not true in all cases, but I definitely wouldn't accept a contract (with any publisher) without making sure I understood my responsibilities. And a few publishers do require the author to do the indexing. I'm not sure if Enslow is one or not. As you get into the educational writing field, you'll hear things about various publishers, and that'll help you know what questions to ask.

HOMEWORK

Fill out the Catalog Analysis Form for at least one of the catalogs you requested and received via mail. If you didn't get a catalog yet, analyze one online. Enslow and some other publishers have downloadable catalogs on their site, so you can download them instantly to your computer (Enslow's online catalog even lets you highlight things and bookmark different things, which is very cool). Please make sure to note the three series that appeal to you!

Catalog Analysis Form

Publisher:

Date of catalog:

Age range:

Subject areas:

One-author series?

Is the look of the books appealing, in general?

Any award-winning books?

Which age range appeals to you most for this publisher?

3 series (multi-author) that appeal to me (length, style, topics, etc.):

1.

2.

3.

Overall impression:

Remember, the goal here is dual: You want to learn more about this particular publisher, but you also are learning how to examine a catalog. If you get through this catalog and decide, "Wow, I have no interest in writing for this company," that's ok! At this point, it's just part of the exercise. If none of the catalogs you requested appeal to you, I would go ahead and order some more. I'm hoping you will soon be able to identify three publishers they'd like to approach.

Here's a Publisher Analysis Form, as well. It's not for you to use as you work through this workbook, but I want to give it to you in case you'd like it for the future. It contains the same info as the Catalog Analysis Form, but it also has a spot to fill out info you know about the publisher, like who you know who's written for them, what you've heard they pay, etc. I think when you're starting out in this field, it's good to have some kind of system (whatever works best for you!) to track this sort of info so it's not overwhelming. That way, as you talk with other writers, you can keep track of the info you get so that you can choose which publishers are the best ones for you to approach.

Publisher Analysis Form

Publisher: Date:

<u>The Books</u>

Imprints/lines:

Age range and word counts:

1)

2)

3)

Subject areas:

High/lows? If so, ages/grade levels/word counts:

Series only?

Style of art (photos, illustrations, color, b/w?):

One–author series?

Imprints or lines I'm interested in:

Particular series that appeal to me:

1)

2)

3)

Making Contact

Guidelines available?

How to contact:

Any personal contact with an editor?

Writing for this Company

Work-for-hire or royalty/advance?

Typical pay:

Payment schedule:

All rights?

Author responsible for art?

Author indexes?

Typical turnaround time?

Who else has written for this company?

1)

2)

3)

FAQ

Tip: I was looking for the word count on a middle grade book in my catalog, but couldn't find it in the Renaissance Learning site. It was supposed to be on the AR list, however. I did a further search and found the Accelerated Reader BookFinder web page (http://www.arbookfind.com). If you click on the book title after the search, you will get the word count.

Tip: There are a couple of supplementary searches that I found useful and thought I might share.

1. Jacketflap.com is a great place for a quick overview, sometimes a blurb about the specific needs of the house, AND whether the house is closed.

2. On Amazon.com, you can search for books by specific publishers in a specific age range (or topic area). This is useful to check out single vs. multi authored series and to see if your topic idea has been done. To do this, generate a book search (on anything). Only then can you see the link to "advanced search." Once there you can put in any parameters you like.

1) *How can you tell if books are written in-house, by the company's staff?*

There's no one sure way to tell. Some publishers whose editors write books for very young kids (like preschool age) have them use pseudonyms. And they don't necessarily want to use in-house writers. It's just that they don't have enough writers with the skill to write for the very young who will do it for the offered pay (which is less and less for very short books). Editors working in this age-range develop a feel for the language and structure and can quickly write them.

Most books like this are still under their real names, though, so you could try doing an Internet search to determine whether the person's an editor. For instance, Jill Kalz, an editor at Picture Window Books, has tons of books with them, too.

http://www.childrensliteraturenetwork.org/aifolder/aipages/ai_k/kalz1.html
http://tinyurl.com/2c8haf8

If you're expressing interest in a series that you suspect is written in-house, you could simply say in your cover letter, "I'm not sure if these Jokes & More Jokes books are written in-house or not, but I love the format and would be interested in writing a book for this series."

That shows you're aware of the possibility and reflects that you are a seasoned, professional writer.

Lesson Four

Topics You Hope to Write About

About this time, some students are usually overwhelmed by the catalogs, so let me say a couple of reassuring things.

First, think of the catalog as a portfolio of the publisher. You are NOT expected to know, understand, and analyze the entire publishing program of each publisher you approach. I've been writing for Capstone and Picture Window Books for years, and I'm sure they have tons of books outside my little area of interest that I'm not even aware of! You just want to analyze it enough to get a sense of whether they're worth approaching. That's all.

Second, you're probably seeing many one-author series. That's fine. It doesn't mean there's not room for you at that publisher. It just means you won't express interest in those series in particular, since they probably aren't assigning them to anyone but that one author.

Third, as far as suggesting a new series vs. writing books for existing series, vs. offering your services up as a writer for any series--you can do any or all of these, and we'll talk about all the options. You can propose series. You can mention books you'd like to write that would fit into existing series. You can just offer to write whatever they need (and that broad approach will get the most results, but you can combine more than one of these). So, don't freak out too much right now about what you're going to say to them. We'll get there. Right now, we're laying the groundwork and familiarizing ourselves with the publishers. The pieces will come together as we continue. I promise :>)

If you feel a little behind or frazzled, don't worry! Don't overwhelm yourself with 8 catalogs (if you've requested and already received tons of them) in one day! Maybe do one per day. That's plenty, really! And today's topic doesn't require you to look at, analyze, study, evaluate, etc., anything except for your own personal history and opinion.

WHAT WILL YOU WRITE ABOUT?

Today we're going to talk about the topics you might want to write about. Does it matter what you want to write about? Didn't I say earlier that the editor picks the topic and assigns it to you?

Yes, I did.

But...your ultimate goal is still to write about things that interest you and/or things you know about, have some expertise in.

You want to write about topics that interest you because it's, well, interesting! Although I always learn fascinating information when I research books, whether the topic is the life cycle of a mealworm or snowmobiling or animal sizes, it's still more fun to write about things you have a natural interest in. For me, anything animal-related (and I'm not really including mealworms, although they are animals) is more interesting than anything history-related.

And you want to write about things you know about because

a) it makes your writing and research easier and
b) it makes you a desirable expert.

CREATING YOUR TOPICS LIST

It's great to be able to list your preferred topics in an introductory packet to your target publisher. It shows the editor some of your personality and also gives her an idea of possible topics to keep you in mind for. You don't have to **limit** yourself to those topics, but it's a starting point to offer up to an editor.

So, what are you an "expert" in? Don't let that word scare you. Just make a word list of things you know about or want to know about. And having some quirky interests in your cover letter can be an excellent thing! Even if it's not something they'll ever write a book about, mentioning that you're an expert in dog treat manufacturing will make your letter a bit more memorable!

During my online classes, as I read 10 or 20 cover letters at once, the lists of people who love animals or biography or eco-topics quickly blurred together. I'm not saying not to include those things. But in addition to your more standard subject areas, throw in a couple of unusual topics. The people who shared that they had experience in a jazz ensemble or loved knock-knock jokes or had lived in Panama as a twine manufacturer—those were the people whose letters I remembered.

Here are some questions to get you started. And as you answer these questions, throw in any other topics that occur to you, even if they don't fit the questions.

What places have you lived?

Where have you visited?

Where have you always dreamed of going?

What kind of weather do you enjoy?

Any weather that fascinates you?

What hobbies have you had?

What hobby do you wish you had the time and/or money to try?

What things frighten you?

What sports have you played? Watched? Coached?

What were your favorite subjects in high school or college?

What jobs have you had?

What's your favorite animal?

What animal terrifies you?

Do you have any phobias?

Who do you admire?

Which period of history would you most like to live in for a month?

What historical figures appeal to you?

What causes do you feel strongly about?

What are three things you want to accomplish before you die?

What is something you wish you could change at your workplace?

What invention are you most grateful for?

What do you wish someone would invent?

What other topics come to mind that interest you?

What questions have you wondered about the answers to?

What questions have your kids/grandkids/students asked you that you didn't know the answer to?

Although it's most likely you'll start out your educational writing career with topics assigned by an editor, it might be that you want to propose titles to fit into existing series or even propose entirely new series. So this word list can also help solidify the areas you're interested in for that purpose.

HOMEWORK

Write your own topics list. In addition to the questions above, you might get ideas from TV listings (I always find topics I'm interested in when I look at Nova and other PBS show listings), magazines, and bookstore shelves. Here's an example of a topics list I put together for myself. This exercise should be fun, not stressful!

My Topics – Interests and Areas of Expertise

Orlando
Working at Walt Disney World
Career as a roller coaster designer/engineer
Atlanta
Scotland
Ireland
Italy
Storms
Hurricanes
Tornadoes
Storms at sea
Origami
Folk painting
Knitting
Paper art
Egg blowing
Wood carving
Jewelry making
Stained glass
Sky diving
Alligators
Volleyball
Racquetball
Trampoline
Gymnastics
Drum corps
Budgeting
Geometry
Clinical psychology
Creative gift-wrapping
Church secretary
Library clerk
Teacher
Nursery grower
Laws of Motion
Space Travel
Space shuttle launches
Challenger disaster
Accounting assistant
Website editor

Newspaper online editor
Magazine editor
Babysitter
Program assistant for people with special needs
Otters
Improv Comedy
Music
Lyric-writing
Whales
Mermaids
Sharks
Grizzly bears
Bugs…big bugs
Renaissance Italy
Ancient Scotland
Edgar Allan Poe
Benjamin Franklin
Madeleine L'Engle
Christopher Columbus
Human rights
Ecology
Education
Travel the world
Whitewater rafting
Gossip
Washer and Dryer
Cleaning robots

Lesson Five

Writing for Different Age Ranges

A little housekeeping work before we get started on this lesson. I'd like you to please obtain at least four books from the SAME SERIES put out by an educational publisher. I don't mean buy them, just get them from the library. It might require a little time (and a little help from your librarian) to find a series published by an educational publisher that your library carries. So it's good to get started on this as quickly as possible to leave a little time for the books to come in from other branches or library systems. You'll need these four books before you can proceed on to the lesson about analyzing a series.

WHAT AGE KIDS WILL YOU WRITE FOR?

Today, we're looking at writing for different age ranges. The purpose of this is to help you think about which age ranges you think you might be good at and naturally suited for. It **doesn't** mean you can only write for one age group! It's just a way to help figure out which age group you might want to try to start with.

If you're not sure what age range you'd like to write for, just be open. A publisher will appreciate your willingness to write for a wide range. But some of you already know you want to write for a certain age. Maybe you teach kids that age. Maybe you have relatives or friends that age. Or maybe you just feel a connection.

And that's ok, too. If you already know you want to write for primary age kids (grades 1–3), for instance, you'll want to share that in your cover letter (more on that soon) and refer to series that are for that age range.

Let's talk a little bit about writing for different age ranges. As I wrote this lesson, I contacted three writer friends, and they each were kind enough to offer a paragraph or two with their thoughts on writing for a specific age group.

WRITING FOR THE PRIMARY GRADES (GRADES K–3)

Writing for kids kindergarten through grade 3 is a real challenge. You have to cut to the heart, figuring out what is most important for children to know and being willing to ruthlessly cut everything else. The limited vocabulary is tough to work with, and you might start feeling repetitive or sing-songy.

The pay is often less for these very short works, although they might require an enormous amount of work. My friend Terri DeGezelle (http://www.terridegezelle.com/) has written many books for this age range, and I recall her struggle to explain the symbolism of the Lincoln Memorial in 500 words.

Here's what Terri had to say:

> Writing for the education market is a great joy. Great joys don't always come easily. Writing nonfiction for young readers can be very difficult, but then I stop and realize I am touching young lives.
>
> Researching a topic as vast as the Lincoln Memorial, for example, can be invigorating and yet be daunting. There comes a point when you must say "Enough. I have to sit down and write." Now, take all the information you've learned and sift, shake, and boil it down and realize you have a 1000-piece word puzzle in front of you but can only use 350 words to make the perfect picture. My task and joy is finding that perfect word from all the words in the world to fill in the blank. Telling a nonfiction story that is neat, concise, entertaining, and all the while educating the reader is truly a work of art.
>
> ---Terri DeGezelle

WRITING FOR THE UPPER ELEMENTARY GRADES (GRADES 4–6)

Writing for the 4th-grade to 7th- or 8th-grade range requires a little bit of information (generally) about a ton of topics. This audience age is good for the generalist.

One problem at this age range, though, is that you go to explain something and then can't really leave it at that. So you find yourself with just enough space to introduce a topic, but not enough to fully explain it. So you end up tiptoeing around so that you don't introduce any questions that are then not answered.

One method I use while writing for this age range is to read my manuscript out loud, and after each sentence or paragraph, I pause to think of what questions a reader might have at that point. Then I read ahead. Do I answer the question? If not, I have a problem and need to reword the original part. I do want to spark readers' interest and hope they'll search out more info about the topic. But the

book needs to stand alone. It can't leave a reader with tons of unanswered questions and lots of frustration.

Another point is that a lot of your research goes unused, and that's OK—in fact, it's necessary.

Here's what Melissa Stewart (http://www.melissa-stewart.com/) wanted to share about writing for this age range:

By the upper elementary grades, children are able to read fairly well on their own. That means I don't have to be as cautious about vocabulary and sentence structure as when I write for beginning readers. Because I can sprinkle dependent clauses throughout the text, the writing flows more naturally. I can also use a wider variety of verbs. Strong verbs really help bring nonfiction writing to life.

Many upper elementary students, especially boys, are fact collectors. They love books full of weird and wacky bits of information, so I included lots of those in books like *Maggots, Grubs, and More: The Secret Lives of Young Insects* (Millbrook, 2003) and *Extreme Nature!* (HarperCollins, 2006).

Upper elementary readers also appreciate nonfiction that reads like a story. In *Baboons* (Lerner, 2007), I include a you–are–there introduction that really pulls readers in and introduces them to the African savanna and the lifestyle of baboons. In *Life in a Wetland* (Lerner, 2003), the entire book is a series of vignettes that together offer an engaging overview of the Florida Everglades ecosystem and its inhabitants.

Finally, I always try to include things that other authors leave out. Reviewers praised my unique, accurate, and clear descriptions in *Butterflies* (NorthWord, 2006). I read a lot about butterflies before I wrote this book, but it was the hours I spent observing them in their natural setting that made all the difference.

---Melissa Stewart

WRITING FOR TEENS (GRADES 7–12)

Writing for teens is very similar to adult writing. You will cover topics in a lot of detail. You do a lot of research, but you will use lots of it. These tend to be longer projects, both in the length of book and in the amount of time you get to write them. I think it's more important, when writing for this age in particular, that you have genuine interest in your topic. Otherwise, it will feel like it's taking forever!

Pat McCarthy shared this about writing educational market books for teens:

Writing for high school and middle school students is a lot like writing for adults. Books are longer and research has to be more in-depth, as does the writing in the books.

You do need to remember that these kids don't have the vocabulary or attention span of an adult, so although your writing is similar to that for adults, you have to be sure to define unfamiliar words and use only those that are necessary for the content. I also am careful to write shorter, simpler sentences than I would for adults.

Older kids are interested in different sorts of information than younger ones, so you need to keep that in mind. In the biographies I did, my publisher wanted me to show both sides, showing the person's faults as well as his or her good points. That means including things like the probability that Henry Ford had an illegitimate son, something I wouldn't have included if the book were for younger children.

Keep in mind that much of what you write for the educational market will be read by kids for reports. Since they often won't be reading your books voluntarily, it's even more important to try to make them interesting. I always am on the lookout for the little tidbit that will fascinate kids. Look for interesting anecdotes and quotes. Teen readers are more demanding than their younger counterparts.

---Pat McCarthy

WHAT IF YOU HAVE A TOPIC, BUT DON'T KNOW FOR WHAT AGE?

If you have a particular topic you want to write about, it can be helpful to know at what age it ties into the curriculum. You can simply ask some teachers, or you can check out standards that describe what students learn when.

For instance, there's a cool database that lets you type in keywords and look for where those words appear in state social studies standards across the country.

http://teachinghistory.org/teaching-materials/state-standards
http://tinyurl.com/7y7pz2k

Let's say I want to write about the Trail of Tears, so I go to that web page and type in Trail of Tears in the search box. Here are the results I get:

http://teachinghistory.org/teaching-materials/state-standards?keys=trail+of+tears&tid=All&tid_1=All

http://tinyurl.com/6rnja7k

I can click on those various links and find out what school kids learn about the Trail of Tears in various grades. I notice that 4th grade is the youngest grade that has standards that include the Trail of Tears, and most of the listings are for secondary grades. That's a very good clue to me that it's unlikely that any educational publisher is going to want to publish a Trail of Tears books for 1st graders. So if that's the topic I want to write about, I need to write for older kids. If I want to write for younger kids, I probably need to propose a different topic.

And here are the national science standards.

http://www.nap.edu/openbook.php?record_id=4962#content.
http://tinyurl.com/2g8cgtl

You have to be more up on educational standards than I am to make sense of those!

Here's the simpler resource I like, the Core Knowledge Sequence for K-8.

http://www.coreknowledge.org/download-the-sequence
http://tinyurl.com/6qlqaup

There, you can download the file for K-8. Or you can buy a printed book version, which is what I have. Basically, it's a proposed system of what kids all over the country would ideally be taught in each grade in each subject area. Our country doesn't necessarily follow this, because each state has the ability to adopt its own standards. But this gives you a great idea of generally what kids are learning at what age. (I actually find this to be a great resource in all of my writing, not just my nonfiction for the educational market.)

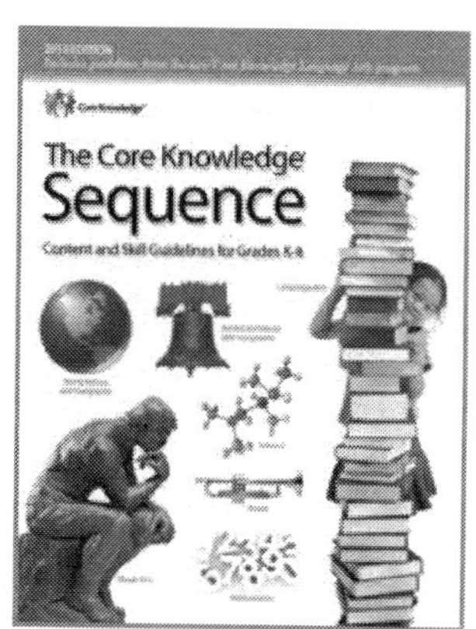

For example, in 2nd grade, in Geography, it lists:

I. Geography
A. SPATIAL SENSE (Working with Maps, Globes, and Other Geographic Tools)
Teachers: Review and reinforce topics from grade 1, including:

- Name your continent, country, state, and community.
- Understand that maps have keys or legends with symbols and their uses.
- Find directions on a map: east, west, north, south.
- Identify major oceans: Pacific, Atlantic, Indian, Arctic.
- The seven continents: Asia, Europe, Africa, North America, South America, Antarctica, Australia.
- Locate: Canada, United States, Mexico, Central America.
- Locate: the Equator, Northern Hemisphere and Southern Hemisphere, North and South Poles.

B. GEOGRAPHICAL TERMS AND FEATURES

Teachers: Review terms from grade 1

It's interesting and incredibly helpful to page through this document and see, generally speaking, what kids of different ages study in school.

CAUTION: Looking at standards can get overwhelming, especially if you don't have a teaching background. If you are open to writing on several different topics, there is no need for you to look at these standards. This is really for if someone wants to write a book, for instance, about how to make your life more eco-friendly. You could look at the standards and it would help you see what aspects of environmentalism are covered at what age. This would help you design a book proposal that presents the topic in an age-appropriate way. 95% of you do not need to worry about looking at standards! So don't go there unless you think you really need to!

HOMEWORK

First, read these 6 samples of the same basic topic covered for various age kids.

1) At the Police Station, by Carol Greene (The Child's World, 1998) 1st–3rd grade, 297 words

(complete text of page 11)

In the dispatch area, officers answer phone calls. They type information from the calls into a computer. Then they radio the information to a patrol card.

Sidebar: Some patrol cars have computer terminals in them. The dispatcher can send information right to them.

2) How Do I Become a…? Police Officer, by Mindi Rose Englart (Thomson/Gale, 2002) 4th–6th grade, 3191 words

(complete text from page 12)

Roll Call

Police officers usually work eight hours in a row. This is called a shift. At the beginning of each shift, a police supervisor takes attendance, or roll call. The captain makes sure all of the officers that are scheduled for the shift have arrived. Then he or she lets them know what to watch out for on the shift. For examples, a captain may announce a bank robbery that happened earlier in the day. He or she gives a description of the robber and hands out a picture that was taken from the bank's security camera. That way, the officers know how to look for the robber.

3) Bomb Detection Squads, by Michael Green (Franklin Watts, 1998) 4th - 6th grade, 2773 words

(one paragraph from page 11)

Chapter Two: Bomb Technicians

Police officers volunteer to serve on bomb squads. Volunteer means to offer to do a job. Officers who want to join bomb squads must be experienced. They must be clever and be able to work well with their hands. They must also be able to deal with the dangers of the job.

4) Undercover Agents (High interest books), by Jil Fine (Children's Press, 2003) 6th grade and higher for reluctant readers, 4045 words

(one paragraph from page 16)

Chapter Two: Taking Off the Uniform

Working in plainclothes is important for undercover police detectives in their fight against crime. All detectives work in plainclothes. This allows them to go places and learn things that a uniformed officer might not. Sometimes police officers on patrol also work in plainclothes to blend in with the crowd. A plainclothes officer is more likely to witness a crime because people don't know that he or she is a police officer.

5) Extreme Careers: Police Swat Teams, by Christopher D. Goranson (Rosen, 2003) 4th–6th grade, 5969 words

(one paragraph from page 11)

Safety, Diligence, and Control

Occupations in the field of law enforcement require the work of qualified, dedicated people. Police officers must display the authority of their positions when dealing with hostile and aggressive people, and hazardous situations. SWAT members must pass physical tests, as one officer's lapse in alertness during a mission can spell trouble—or even disaster—for the entire team. They must also pass intelligence tests.

6) Guide to Law Enforcement Careers, by Donald B. Hutton and Anna Mydlarz (Barron's, 1997) adult, 344 pages

(one paragraph from page 18)

General Law Enforcement Requirements

With the above general duties in mind, the rationale for certain requirements from candidates becomes clear. Listed below are a somewhat universal list of law enforcement requirements, however, (sic) every agency has it's (sic) own set of qualification standards. Candidates should use the following only as a guideline and contact each agency directly for exact requirements, which vary and change with time.

<u>Second</u>, take about an hour and write about your job or a job you know something about. You're going to write it for three different age ranges. For each, write your information in a way that your imagined audience could understand. Don't worry about facts right now—just make them up if you need to! This exercise is about writing style and voice, **not** about research.

Here are your **three assignments**.

For a K–3 child, write 4–5 short sentences about your job as you would describe it to a 6-year-old, making sure that each sentence could support an illustration. Try to use very simple vocabulary and cover <u>all</u> the main duties of this job.

For a grade 4–6 child, write a paragraph of 4–5 sentences aimed at a 9-year-old. Define the job, describe the training required, and talk about the skills required for the job.

For a 9th-grader, write a paragraph (5–6 sentences) aimed at a 15-year-old studying careers. In your paragraph, introduce the career and indicate what kind of kid it might appeal to.

Remember, make up the facts if you want! Then ask yourself a few questions:

- How did it go?
- Which age range felt the most comfortable for you? Why?
- Which felt the hardest to write? Why?
- Do you have a specific age range you hope to write for, or are you open to several possibilities?

FAQ

1) *What do you do about gender when you're writing about a made-up example of a person?*

The publisher almost always has a policy for you to follow. Sometimes it's to use plural forms. For instance, you could say, "Police officers help people. They try to keep the streets and parks safe for kids." Other times, a book follows one person the entire time, so the gender stays the same. Other times, they ask you to alternate: "A police officer has various duties. He responds to the scene when someone is committing a crime." And so on. And then your next paragraph might be: "A police officer typically has some training after high school. She might have a college degree in criminology, or perhaps she has graduated from the police academy." It varies, so you'll want to follow the example of the other books in the series and/or double-check with your editor.

Lesson Six

The Introductory Packet

Before starting this lesson, I'd like you to look back at your own age-range passages and think about a couple things, just to evaluate how you think you did.

First, did you follow directions? Did you write the assigned number of sentences? The number one, most important rule for educational writing on assignment is to follow the guidelines/directions the editor gives you. I'll talk about guidelines and I'll show you some samples later in the class. They vary in their explicitness. But I've been given directions as explicit as 3-4 sentences per spread. So you have to be able to read, understand, and follow directions really well. If the editor asks for 6 sentences and you give her 10, she will be unhappy. Trust me.

Second, did you maintain a tight focus? It's very hard to follow these directions, especially the ones for grades 4-6 and 7-9. I'm asking for a lot of info in a very tight space. And that's common. Publishers must pack as much information as possible into their books, and sometimes their requests seem almost impossible. It's your job to make it work. And it won't be impossible. But it will require you to find the essence of your topic. What ABSOLUTELY MUST be in this passage, this page, this chapter? You will constantly be leaving things out you think should be included.

I think about teaching a foreign language. When I took Spanish I, I'm sure we all sounded like blithering idiots trying to speak Spanish in the classroom. But Señora Everson didn't worry about that. She didn't try to teach us EVERYTHING about Spanish that year. Instead, she lay down a baseline amount of information. Information that was somewhat useful (Does anyone want to go to la biblioteca today?), but that certainly wouldn't make us experts. But as we learned and were ready to learn more, we needed that baseline info. That's how educational market books are. You won't be able to share everything you want to share about a topic. So an important skill will be teasing out the info that's **most** important and most interesting to share.

Third, how was your voice? Different series have different voices, and we'll talk more about that later. But in general, a conversational tone works well. So, read each passage out loud, and this time, imagine you're actually reading it to a real, live kid in your target audience age range. Does it feel natural? Did you use a casual, conversational tone? Have you included details and concrete images that kids can understand and relate to?

If you checked the readability of your piece, and it was high, don't panic. (And if you don't even know what readability is at this point, that's absolutely fine!) I'll talk more about readability later, and you'll learn how to use the samples a publisher provides to make sure your book is on target! However, if your K–3 passage had a readability of 9th grade or something, that's definitely an issue that would have to be addressed.

WHAT EXACTLY IS AN INTRODUCTORY PACKET?

OK, on to today's topic: the infamous **Introductory Packet**, which I keep mentioning!

The introductory packet is just what it sounds like. It's a way to introduce yourself to a publisher and whichever particular editor you send it to. It is basically a job application.

With educational writing, you are writing on assignment, writing exactly what the publisher is looking for. The purpose of the introductory packet is to convince the editor that you are professional, competent, and easy to work with.

Here are the possible components of the introductory packet. I'll talk in more detail about each of these components over the next few lessons.

Cover letter – ALWAYS include a cover letter. Use it to introduce yourself, share any writing or subject-matter experience/expertise, show that you're professional, and make a connection with the editor. Share a little enthusiasm and personality, but keep it professional!

Publications list – Include this only if you have more than 3 or 4 writing credits. If you have a few credits, just include them in your cover letter. If you have none, don't mention that at all.

Résumé – If you have work experience that is relevant (editing, publishing, teaching, working in the field that you want to write about), include a résumé.

Clips – Clips can be published or unpublished. Always send something aimed at kids. You should definitely send clips with your introductory packet if you're unpublished. If you're published, you could send them then, or you could simply offer to send them.

Business card – Get one! They're cheap.

SASE or reply postcard – Always include this!

DECIDING WHAT TO SEND

So how do you know which pieces to send? Well, you should ***always*** include a cover letter and an SASE or a reply postcard. Everything else depends. What does it depend on?

First, you should check for writers' guidelines at the websites of publishers you're interested in approaching. Some are very general. Some tell you to email for guidelines. Others are fairly specific. So if you are able to find writers' guidelines, or if you hear an editor speak or you read an interview with an editor (I always do an online search for interviews with a company's editors before submitting an introductory packet), then follow those directions!

But on many sites, I find no guidelines at all. In those cases, I use the above components. I do a cover letter, and I send them to my website for my publications list.

http://www.laurasalas.com/pdfs/Other/Book%20List.pdf
http://tinyurl.com/2ftk2zz

I also enclose a résumé with my teaching and editorial experience, mention the availability of clips, and send a business card and a reply postcard.

FINDING EDITORS

When addressing your cover letter, it's always better if you can find a specific name rather than a title, like Submissions Editor or something. You're likely to get read faster and by someone higher up (someone who can actually make assignments) if you send it to a specific editor.

Here are some resources I might use to find a specific name:

- Search Google with terms like "Rosen Publishing" and "editor"
- Ask on the NFforKids list
- Call the publisher directly and ask for the name of an editor who reviews introductory packets, but not manuscripts, from potential writers
- I might already have a name from various newsletters I get (see the Resources List at the back of the book)

HOMEWORK

Choose 2 or 3 publishers to whom you're going to submit introductory packets. Perhaps you've already identified, through studying catalogs, several publishers who put out books you would enjoy writing. Great! Simply choose from those.

If you have not yet found 2 or 3 that appeal to you, explore the websites of various publishers. (Or go to a public or school library and find some educational publishers whose books appeal to you.) I.D. the publishers that you would like to send your packets to.

NOTE: If you're waiting for more catalogs by snail mail and you dislike evaluating publishers online, that's fine. You can just wait until you receive the catalogs.

Remember, you are <u>not</u> making any legal commitment by sending an introductory packet. Sometimes writers want to wait to send these because they are pregnant, or overwhelmed with family duties, or have other writing projects at the moment. But it can take months (sometimes years!) to get a response from an editor. So don't wait until you want the assignment. Send that packet now! When you send an introductory packet, the best result is an editor calling or emailing to discuss an assignment. You can always refuse any assignment that doesn't appeal to you or doesn't fit your schedule, or doesn't pay enough…or that you simply don't want!

Once you have chosen your publishers, search online for both writers' guidelines and editor names. If you can't find this information, don't panic. I rarely spend more than 15 minutes looking for guidelines and editor name combined. It WILL become easier with time and practice! Don't stress out about it. Simply vow to search for one each on the three next days.

Don't move on to the next lesson until you have your three publisher names, editor names (if at all possible), and submission guidelines (if available).

FAQ

1) *What is a headlist? One publisher asked for a book proposal, including sample chapters and a headlist.*

Wow, I've never even heard of a headword list. Doing a little research, it appears to be a listing of all the topics covered in a book--almost like an index, but without page numbers.

http://ventumusa.com/IR/documents/IR%20Headword%20List%20(complete).pdf
http://tinyurl.com/2a6gdts

I've never seen a request for one before!

As far as sample chapters...ugh. If you are new to educational writing, it's likely they will ask for a proposal if it's a book for older kids/teens. These are generally for books with a deadline of 6 months to 1 year. Otherwise, publishers mostly don't have time to mess with proposals. I did do a proposal for my very first book (and I had done a proposal for a different series for the same editor, and that's what impressed her), but I haven't had to do one since.

Unless you want to write for very young kids, you might well have to write a proposal to get your first go-ahead. But it annoys me that some publishers insist you submit "a proposal" blindly. It's like your audition. If you're willing to do it, go for it. I will only do one on a topic the publisher requests one on! But that's just me. Plenty of people do break in by doing a proposal, and then the editor calls and says, "Well, we don't need that book, but would you like to write about the history of covered wagons?" Or whatever.

If a publisher asks you to submit a proposal as an audition, I personally would offer to do a proposal on a book of their choice and see if that works...If it's a book on a topic you know they want, then if you do a good job on the proposal, the job is yours!

2) *There's a series I love, but every book is written by one person. Do I have a chance?*

That is so disappointing, I know! And it never hurts to mention how much you love that series, even though you realize it's a one-author series. Tell them you'd enjoy working on something similar because it's so fantastic. I've been asked to step in to take over a one-author series when the author had health issues or got tired of writing the books. So it's always possible, but the chances are pretty darn small, unfortunately.

3) *What if there's a publisher I really want to write for, and they don't respond to my introductory packet?*

Be persistent. It took me a couple of years to break into Picture Window Books. Meanwhile, I was writing for other companies, but I kept touching base with PWB, and I finally got a call and an assignment to write 6 books. I *really* like their books, and that's the only reason I was so persistent. If they had been on my so-so list, I probably would've moved on earlier. But if it's a publisher you love, you should keep on trying. I've written many Picture Window Books over the past 7 years, so that persistence paid off. But even while you're following-up with your top choice publisher, approach and write for other publishers. Getting some current publishing credits will only make you more appealing to your top choice publisher.

Lesson Seven

The Cover Letter

The cover letter is the first impression you make upon an editor, so it's very important. But it's really not that difficult to write. We just place so much attention on it that it becomes intimidating.

Here are some tips for writing a great cover letter:

Use business letter format.

http://writing.wisc.edu/Handbook/BusLetter_Block.html
http://tinyurl.com/yj7vqjy

Find an individual editor to address your letter to.

Keep your letter to one single-spaced page.

In the first paragraph, **explain why you are contacting the editor**. Also mention if you've had any contact with that editor. If you're responding to a call for writers, this is the place to mention it. A call for writers is when a publisher is actively seeking writers for current projects. Sometimes people on email lists will share stuff like this. Most often, I see calls for writers in various newsletters. See the resource list at the back of this book for a couple of newsletters that frequently feature educational writing notices.

In other paragraphs, try to accomplish these objectives:

Share your areas of interest and expertise, either by simply listing them and/or through publication credits and/or résumé. Here is where you might list anywhere from 3–10 areas of interest (depending on space) from your topics list that you made earlier. It's great to choose a few broader topics that obviously fit into educational publishing as well as a few more unique topics that might not be immediately applicable to educational publishing but that show a bit of your own personality. That helps make the list more memorable.

NOTE: If you have a very specific area you would like to write about, tell the editor your topic of choice and mention which series you think the topic could work within. Or propose a brand new series on the topic (more on this soon), and offer to send a brief proposal if she has any interest.

Let the editor know you have researched the company. A reference to a few series you particularly like will do the trick.

Present yourself as professional. Convince the editor that you have good skills like meeting deadlines, working to specifications, etc.

Let the editor know how she can contact you. If you have letterhead, great. If not, make sure your address, phone number, and email are all easy to find in your letter.

Invite the editor to contact you to discuss assignments.

Thank the editor for his or her time.

It's really that simple. If you can inject a little of your personality into the letter, even better. But while a touch of humor can be appropriate (especially if you've had any prior contact with the editor) and help your cover letter stand out, make sure you still keep the tone of the letter professional.

I've found that students seem to have an especially hard time with that very first paragraph. This cover letter is like a cold sales call, so that very first sentence can be tough. Here are **just a few opening sentences** I've used over the years when cold-calling on an editor:

- I'm a freelance children's writer, and I'd love to write for your company.
- I have been studying your catalog, and I would love to write for your company.
- I'm a children's writer who is interested in writing for your company.

- As a freelance children's writer, I have studied many educational publishers' catalogs.
- I've been studying your catalog and reading some of your titles, and I'm so impressed.

OK, that's just a few of them. But you get the idea. There's no magic to it. And it can sometimes sound a bit awkward. Just try to convey that you have a valid reason for contacting them. And you do!

Here are a few of my early cover letters.

Laura Purdie Salas
123 Main St. * Anytown, MN 55428
555-555-5555 * lpsalas@email.com
www.laurasalas.com

Today's Date

Chandra Howard, Acquisitions Editor
Lucent Books & Kidhaven Press
10911 Technology Place
San Diego, CA 92127

Dear Ms. Howard: [Use standard business letter form and punctuation]

A couple of years ago, I queried you about a series proposal and you let me know that you develop all titles in-house. You also kindly invited me to request a new author packet if I was interested in writing on assignment. [Make a connection] I had several other projects in the works at the time and didn't pursue it, but I'm wondering if that offer still stands.

I have been writing children's nonfiction for several years, and I have never missed a deadline. I enjoy learning about new topics and then passing along that information to kids. My favorite subjects are the natural sciences, but I've written about sports, countries, history, and famous people. I always find intriguing facts in my research, even on topics I'm not initially thrilled about! [Tell a little about yourself]

I have written nonfiction books for several publishers, including Lerner, Capstone, Steck-Vaughn, and Child Welfare League of America. Please visit my web page for a complete listing of my writing credits. [Share writing credits]

I am a former magazine editor and English teacher. I work part-time as an online editor for the Minneapolis *Star Tribune*, and I am an active member of SCBWI and the Children's Literature Network. [Offer any related credentials]

I am most interested in writing books for KidHaven series, as I prefer to write for younger readers. I am especially interested in the following series: Extreme Places, Nature's Predators, Wonders of the World, and KidHaven Science Library. Several other series, such as Creatures of the Sea and Animals with Jobs, look like such fun to write for, but I see they are single-author series. [Show you've researched the publisher] I'd also be open to the possibility of writing for other series in the science and social studies areas.

Can you send me a new author packet? Or would you be interested in discussing possible assignments? [Ask a question that invites response] I am enclosing a reply postcard, but please feel free to e-mail me or call me at xxx-xxx-xxxx. I look forward to hearing from you, and thanks for your consideration.

Sincerely,

Laura Purdie Salas

Laura Purdie Salas
***
9000 Main Street * Minneapolis, MN 55369
Phone: xxx-xxx-xxxx * E-mail: LPSalas@juno.com

Today's Date

Lois Wallentine
Product Development/Editorial Manager
Capstone Press
6117 Blue Circle Drive, #150
Minnetonka, MN 55343

Dear Lois:

It was a pleasure to meet you at the SCBWI conference. I enjoyed chatting with you throughout the day, and I liked learning more about Capstone Press.

You asked prospective authors to describe their interests and topics of expertise, but I'll have to settle for interests. I'm not an expert in any particular area, but my interests are far-ranging (that explains my ever-changing major in college!). I am most interested in animals, nature, science, history, health, anthropology, the arts, and anyone whose life makes a great story. I love to learn new things. For example, a paragraph in a murder mystery sparked my interest in Mt. Everest and the seabed rock cycle. I started researching it, and the result was Seashells in the Sky, an article I'm currently trying to place. I've enclosed a copy of it as one of my writing samples. I also did fairly extensive research recently on both fireworks and the history of swimwear. I enjoy learning unexpected facts and seeing how the past connects to the present.

I would love to write a book for Capstone Press. The Pebble, Bridgestone and Capstone imprints most closely fit my interests and writing style. I'm not sure exactly which series are open to new authors since I see many series have only one author for all the books.

I am enclosing a resume, writing samples and references. If you would like to see any more samples of my writing, published or unpublished, please let me know. I think I'd be a good fit for Capstone because I enjoy learning about new subjects and passing that knowledge on to kids in an easy to understand manner. I am extremely reliable and have never missed a deadline for a writing assignment. I have no problem working within very specific guidelines; in fact, I prefer that. That way I know exactly what is expected of me, and I can be sure that I'm providing the information the editor wants.

Please contact me if you'd like more information or would like to discuss a project. I hope to talk with you soon.

Sincerely,

Laura Purdie Salas

Laura Purdie Salas
8000 Main Street, Minneapolis, MN 55000 * xxx-xxx-xxxx
lpsalas@email.net * http://www.ourcreativespace.com/laurasalas/

Today's Date

Paul Abdo, Editor in Chief,
ABDO Publishing
4940 Viking Drive, Ste. 622
Edina, MN 55435

Dear Mr. Abdo:

I'm writing to express interest in working with you on nonfiction books. Let me tell you a little bit about my background. I'm a former 8th-grade English teacher, and I have a background in both writing and editing. I have been a magazine editor and a freelance writer, and I work part-time as an online editor at the *Star Tribune.*

For the past several years, I have concentrated on writing for children. I have written nine books (many of them high-lows) for Capstone Press. I have one Creative Minds biography (on Isaac Newton) out with Lerner Publishing. I wrote a leveled-reading nonfiction book for Steck-Vaughn as part of their Power Up! middle school reading series, and I have a nonfiction self-help book for teens coming out from Child Welfare League of America next spring. I have sold fiction, nonfiction, and poetry to several magazines and educational publishers and I have several picture books (fiction and nonfiction) making the rounds.

I am an instructor with the Institute of Children's Literature, and I also teach children's writing courses at the Loft Literary Center in Minneapolis. Please see my website for additional background information: http://www.ourcreativespace.com/laurasalas/.

I am currently working on expanding my publisher base. I am a professional writer, and I meet my deadlines and work well with editors. I'd be happy to provide you with some editors you can call for references if you'd like.

I am most interested in writing for the Sandcastle or Buddy Books lines. I can take on an entire series (depending on my workload at that time) or I am happy to write individual titles for an existing series. Nature and science would be my preferred areas, but I would be pleased to write history or biography books, as well. I'm also interested in writing on social issues (self-esteem, social skills, friendship, etc.) and health/mental health issues.

Please contact me by e-mail or phone if you have any questions or would like to discuss this further. Thanks for your time and consideration.

Sincerely,

Laura Purdie Salas

So, cover letters aren't as hard as you thought! However, here are a few things to **avoid** doing in your cover letter, mostly because they make the editor think you're an amateur, which is exactly the opposite of the impression you're hoping to make.

Things NOT to do in your cover letter:

Enclose teabags, chocolate, or anything cute.

Invite the editor to meet you in person.

Ask if you can call the editor.

State that you've never written a book before.

Mention how much your children/grandchildren/students love your writing.

HOMEWORK

Pick one of your three chosen publishers and write a rough draft of a cover letter that will be part of your introductory packet.

Don't freak out about this. If you know your publisher, have studied and liked the catalog, etc., you can likely write your cover letter in an hour or less.

If you feel inspired and have several publishers already chosen, go ahead and write cover letters for them, as well. The bulk of the letters will be the same, but **each letter should have a few sentences specific to that publisher.** Make sure you change those sentences, or you'll be very embarrassed to receive a note from an editor pointing out that they are not the publisher of the series you listed. Yikes.

FAQ

1) *If I have my books or works listed at Jacketflap.com, can I send editors there?*

While it's probably not quite as effective as a website, because you can't control the display of it, I think that would be just fine.

Make sure to send them directly to the url—don't just say: You can view my books at jacketflap.com. Instead, say, You can see my books listed at jacketflap.com at

http://www.jacketflap.com/work.asp?member=salaslp
http://tinyurl.com/2cojwrk

Editors don't have time to search for you on a site, so make it as easy as possible for them.

A site like jacketflap.com is one way to have a public presence. I've also been a member of the Children's Literature Network for years, and once you have a published book, that can be a nice, professional-looking online presence without having to invest the time in creating and maintaining your own site. You can see my page there.

http://www.childrensliteraturenetwork.org/aifolder/aipages/ai_s/salas.php
http://tinyurl.com/7rtrcxa

Another option I'm liking is Wordpress.com. I have my blog at Wordpress.com (http://laurasalas.wordpress.com), but many writers use it for their actual website. You can create various pages (like my About Me, My Half.com Store, etc., pages), choose from various themes/looks, and personalize it in many ways. You do NOT have to become a blogger to do this. Your Home Page can just be static (unchanging), like the homepage of a website. Wordpress is free.

Lesson Eight

The Rest of the Introductory Packet

Now, your cover letter isn't the only thing you send. Here's a roundup of the rest of the possible components of your introductory packet—**except** for writing samples/clips! We'll work on that in the next lesson.

PUBLICATIONS LIST

You already know that if you have no publications, that's ok. Just don't mention it in your cover letter.

If you have five or fewer published works (including books, magazines, newspaper pieces, etc.), I would simply name a few of them in your cover letter. Your paragraph might read something like this:

"I have been writing for children and adults for several years. My work has been published in various markets, including *The Maple Grove Courier*, *Minnesota Parent* magazine, and *New Moon for Children*."

If you have numerous publication credits, whether they are for kids or for adults, you might want to include a publication list. I have my publications list available online.

http://www.laurasalas.com/pdfs/Other/Book%20List.pdf
http://tinyurl.com/2ftk2zz

I rarely send a hard copy, but I do send the link when approaching an editor I haven't worked with before.

RÉSUMÉ

I only include a résumé in my introductory packet in two cases.

1) If the publisher's submissions guidelines say to send a résumé.

2) If I have work experience that I think makes me an extra good fit for a publisher. This work experience could include teaching experience, writing or editing staff positions, and work in a specific field (as an engineer, for instance, if I want to write about science topics).

You can use a traditional chronological résumé or a functional résumé, where you group your skills into categories. There are plenty of résumé -writing sites, such as this one at about.com.

http://jobsearch.about.com/od/resumes/a/aa040801a.htm
http://tinyurl.com/2zxhwg

Microsoft Word also can walk you right through the process of writing your résumé. Simply choose File-New. Somewhere on the screen that loads (it depends which version of Word you're using), there will be résumé templates to choose from.

Here's an outdated functional résumé for me.

LAURA PURDIE SALAS
5000 Main Street
Minneapolis, MN 55000
www.laurasalas.com
E-mail: lpsalas@bitstream.net
xxx-xxx-xxxx

OBJECTIVE:
Fiction, nonfiction, and poetry writing assignments

WRITING SKILLS:
Write fiction, nonfiction and poetry for children (see my website at www.laurasalas.com)
Write children's nonfiction books to match series guidelines
Write testing passages and questions for educational standardized tests
Meet editor-specified length, reading level, interest level, and structure
Research accurately and balance information
Write occasional feature/travel stories for Star Tribune

EDITING SKILLS:
Copyedit stories for startribune.com
Proof/copyedit highlights pages for startribune.com
Copyedited textbooks for Harcourt Brace Jovanovich
Edited student materials as an instructor for the Institute of Children's Literature (ICL)
Worked as a freelance copyeditor for Fanfare magazine
Assigned and edited stories as staff editor for two magazines

OTHER SKILLS:
Teach/speak on children's writing for The Loft Literary Center and the Society of Children's Book Writers and Illustrators
Work efficiently and meet deadlines in all my projects
Work independently with minimal supervision
Taught basic writing skills to students of ICL
Taught 8th-grade English for two years

EDUCATION:
B.A. in English (emphasis in Creative Writing), University of Central Florida, July 1987

RECENT EMPLOYMENT HISTORY:
Part-time editor, startribune.com, 1997 - present
Freelance writer and editor, 1990 - present
Instructor, Institute of Children's Literature, 2002 - 2004

References available upon request

I've created loads of different résumés over the years, often just varying one slightly to emphasize the skills or experience or education that I think will be the most meaningful to the particular publisher I'm sending to. So I'd suggest having a base file that you call resume.doc. Then every time you tweak it for a particular publisher, use Save As and give it a different name, like Ens_Res_081511. That way you'll have a record of the résumé you sent Enslow on August 15, 2011. Or whatever. This makes it easier to find your various résumé files if you want to use the same one again. And if Enslow comes calling, you can look at your résumé to see exactly which of your skills you emphasized and that they might be expecting to talk about.

BUSINESS CARD

I strongly suggest a business card. I would include it in your introductory packet and keep a few handy in your wallet to hand out to people you meet.

What should your card have on it? Basically, your name and a way to contact you, along with an identification of you as a children's writer. It's that simple.

I have always used vistaprint.com for my business cards. They have a lot of templates, and if you use a basic template (they have many to choose from), the cost is less than $6 for 250 cards, shipped. Even the ones where you choose premium designs are fairly inexpensive. I've had various designs over the years. I did a custom one a couple of years ago, using a bit of an illustration (http://www.laurasalas.com/poetry.html) that artist Liz Jones (http://lizjonesbooks.livejournal.com/) did for my website.

Then I had:

And my most recent business card had my **Stampede**! cover on the front, with the title, my name and the illustrator's name, and the publisher and year. And on the back, I had a bit of spot art from the book plus a black bar with my website address. That's it.

Front (the fronts of all of these cards were in color, by the way)

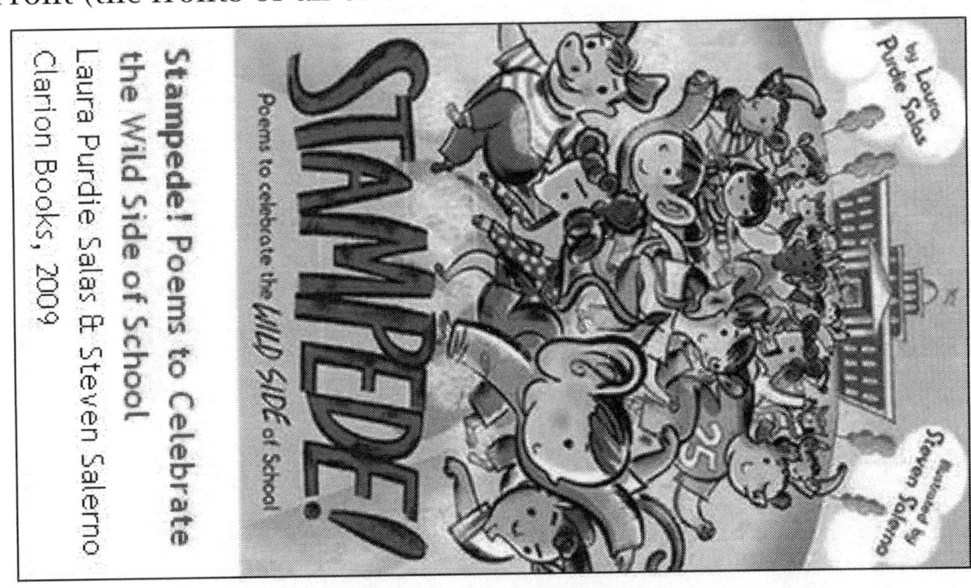

Back (which is in black and white):

As I write this, I have on my to-do list for this month—New business cards! I need to figure out what approach I want to take next. With three trade books out (and those are the ones I emphasize since they are advance-and-royalty), I might go back to a less image-based card. Maybe I'll do my name, website, blog, and just a bit of spot art from one of my newest books. I'll have to go to vistaprint.com and play around with some possibilities.

And as I proofread this, I have ordered my cards. Here's my latest version, which does use a bit of spot art I love from BOOKSPEAK! POEMS ABOUT BOOKS (Clarion, 2011). Here's the front:

Laura Purdie Salas
poet, writer, mentor, teacher
SELECTED TITLES
A Leaf Can Be... (Millbrook Press, 2012)
BookSpeak! Poems About Books (Clarion, 2011)
Stampede! Poems to Celebrate the Wild Side of School (Clarion, 2009)

And here's the back:

site: laurasalas.com
blog: laurasalas.wordpress.com
© 2011
Josée Bisaillon
BookSpeak!

I stopped putting my phone number and address on my cards. Editors are all very web–savvy, and I heard enough cautionary tales and dealt with one annoying/scary person. That was enough to convince me not to hand out my info so freely. Of course, a determined person could track me down in 10 minutes on the web, but I decided to at least not hand them paper with my address/phone number on it! I can always jot my number or email address on the card when handing it to an editor, if I want to.

It's totally your choice, though. Many people still have their address and phone number on their cards. I just ask that you give it some thought if the phone number and address are your home ones.

SASE or REPLY POSTCARD

Standard protocol is to include a self-addressed, stamped envelope whenever you send anything to an editor. To do that, you would simply take a #10 standard business envelope and put your name and address or place an address sticker in the To: area of the envelope. Then, in the upper left corner, you would write the name of the publisher you're approaching. That way, when you get a response in that envelope, you'll know who it's from. Editors don't always sign their notes! And even when they do, that signature might not be legible :>) Then pop a first-class stamp on the envelope and you're good to go.

I do something a little different. I use a reply postcard. I go to the post office and buy stamped blank postcards. In Word, I have a file that has my checklist on it. I print out my postcards, and the result looks like this.

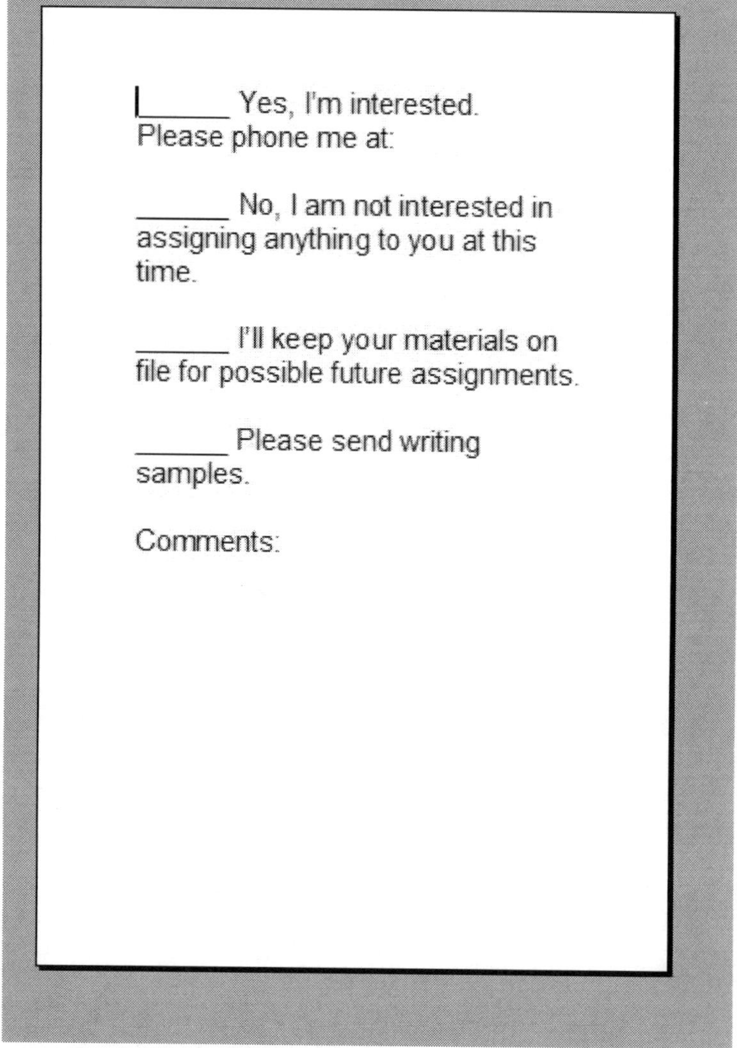

______ Yes, I'm interested.
Please phone me at:

______ No, I am not interested in assigning anything to you at this time.

______ I'll keep your materials on file for possible future assignments.

______ Please send writing samples.

Comments:

On the other side, which already has the stamp, I put an address label for me in the To: area, and then I put the publisher info in the upper left corner, like this:

ENSLOW
INTRO100408

When I get that postcard back in the mail, I know that I sent Enslow an introductory packet on October 4, 2008, and this postcard is in response to that.

I've gotten nice feedback from editors on these postcards; many seem to like the simplicity of them. But either method, envelope or postcard, is just fine.

Also, because you'll be including writing samples unless you have several books out already, your postcard list would perhaps include, "Please send **more** writing samples."

Directions for Creating the Printed Postcard in Word 2010

In Microsoft Word 2010, I open a new file, and then go to Page Layout-Size. Then I choose More Paper Sizes, then Paper-Paper Size-Custom. I make the paper 3.4" x 5", and I set the margins at .4" for top and bottom, and .5" for left and right. I choose Manual Feed.

Then I enter whatever text I want, and I print them out. I usually have to hand feed the postcards one at a time in the Manual Feed area of my printer. If you're planning to do many submissions, I recommend printing out 25-50 at a time, so you only have to mess with it every few months.

HOMEWORK

If you do not already have business cards, visit vistaprint.com or the business card creator of your choice and create a business card for yourself.

FAQ

1) *I am struggling a little with how to organize my information/activities. For example, I thought I ordered catalogs of everything on the list that you sent initially. I've not received all of them, but I'm not positive I ordered them all. Do you recommend keeping some kind of business journal that tracks what you do each day?*

I don't keep track of what I do every day in a prose format, but I do track all contact with editors. I use Excel spreadsheets to do this. I have columns for publisher, editor, what I sent, when I sent it, what answer I got, when I want to follow up, etc. It depends what info you want to keep track of. So...yes, I do recommend keeping track of your writing activities (whether for the educational market, or any other kind of writing you're trying to sell). The form you keep it in is up to you. You can use a handwritten form, a spreadsheet...whatever works for you.

Here's a screenshot of my database.

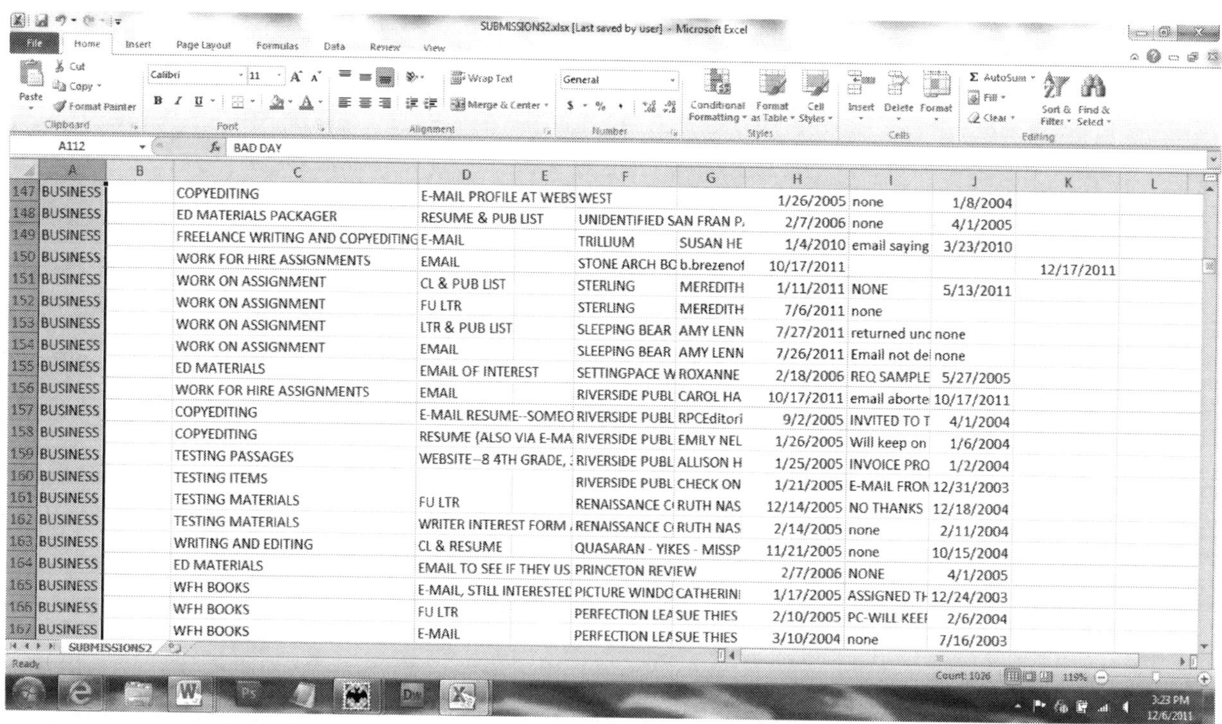

	A	B	C	D	E	F	G	H	I	J	K	L
147	BUSINESS		COPYEDITING	E-MAIL PROFILE AT WEBS		WEST		1/26/2005	none	1/8/2004		
148	BUSINESS		ED MATERIALS PACKAGER	RESUME & PUB LIST		UNIDENTIFIED SAN FRAN P.		2/7/2006	none	4/1/2005		
149	BUSINESS		FREELANCE WRITING AND COPYEDITING	E-MAIL		TRILLIUM	SUSAN HE	1/4/2010	email saying	3/23/2010		
150	BUSINESS		WORK FOR HIRE ASSIGNMENTS	EMAIL		STONE ARCH BC	b.brezenof	10/17/2011			12/17/2011	
151	BUSINESS		WORK ON ASSIGNMENT	CL & PUB LIST		STERLING	MEREDITH	1/11/2011	NONE	5/13/2011		
152	BUSINESS		WORK ON ASSIGNMENT	FU LTR		STERLING	MEREDITH	7/6/2011	none			
153	BUSINESS		WORK ON ASSIGNMENT	LTR & PUB LIST		SLEEPING BEAR	AMY LENN	7/27/2011	returned unc	none		
154	BUSINESS		WORK ON ASSIGNMENT	EMAIL		SLEEPING BEAR	AMY LENN	7/26/2011	Email not del	none		
155	BUSINESS		ED MATERIALS	EMAIL OF INTEREST		SETTINGPACE W	ROXANNE	2/18/2006	REQ SAMPLE	5/27/2005		
156	BUSINESS		WORK FOR HIRE ASSIGNMENTS	EMAIL		RIVERSIDE PUBL	CAROL HA	10/17/2011	email aborte	10/17/2011		
157	BUSINESS		COPYEDITING	E-MAIL RESUME--SOMEO		RIVERSIDE PUBL	RPCEditori	9/2/2005	INVITED TO T	4/1/2004		
158	BUSINESS		COPYEDITING	RESUME (ALSO VIA E-MA		RIVERSIDE PUBL	EMILY NEL	1/26/2005	Will keep on	1/6/2004		
159	BUSINESS		TESTING PASSAGES	WEBSITE--8 4TH GRADE, :		RIVERSIDE PUBL	ALLISON H	1/25/2005	INVOICE PRO	1/2/2004		
160	BUSINESS		TESTING ITEMS			RIVERSIDE PUBL	CHECK ON	1/21/2005	E-MAIL FRON	12/31/2003		
161	BUSINESS		TESTING MATERIALS	FU LTR		RENAISSANCE C	RUTH NAS	12/14/2005	NO THANKS	12/18/2004		
162	BUSINESS		TESTING MATERIALS	WRITER INTEREST FORM ,		RENAISSANCE C	RUTH NAS	2/14/2005	none	2/11/2004		
163	BUSINESS		WRITING AND EDITING	CL & RESUME		QUASARAN - YIKES - MISSP		11/21/2005	none	10/15/2004		
164	BUSINESS		ED MATERIALS	EMAIL TO SEE IF THEY US		PRINCETON REVIEW		2/7/2006	NONE	4/1/2005		
165	BUSINESS		WFH BOOKS	E-MAIL, STILL INTERESTEC		PICTURE WINDC	CATHERINI	1/17/2005	ASSIGNED TH	12/24/2003		
166	BUSINESS		WFH BOOKS	FU LTR		PERFECTION LEA	SUE THIES	2/10/2005	PC-WILL KEEI	2/6/2004		
167	BUSINESS		WFH BOOKS	E-MAIL		PERFECTION LEA	SUE THIES	3/10/2004	none	7/16/2003		

2) *How do you keep track of information on publishers?*

I also keep a publishers database. I have the name, who I heard about them from, what date I heard of them, an editor's name, notes about what they publish, and what my action I want to do is. I don't actually refer to this too much, but I still keep it. It does come in handy when I'm doing publisher research for my trade manuscripts!

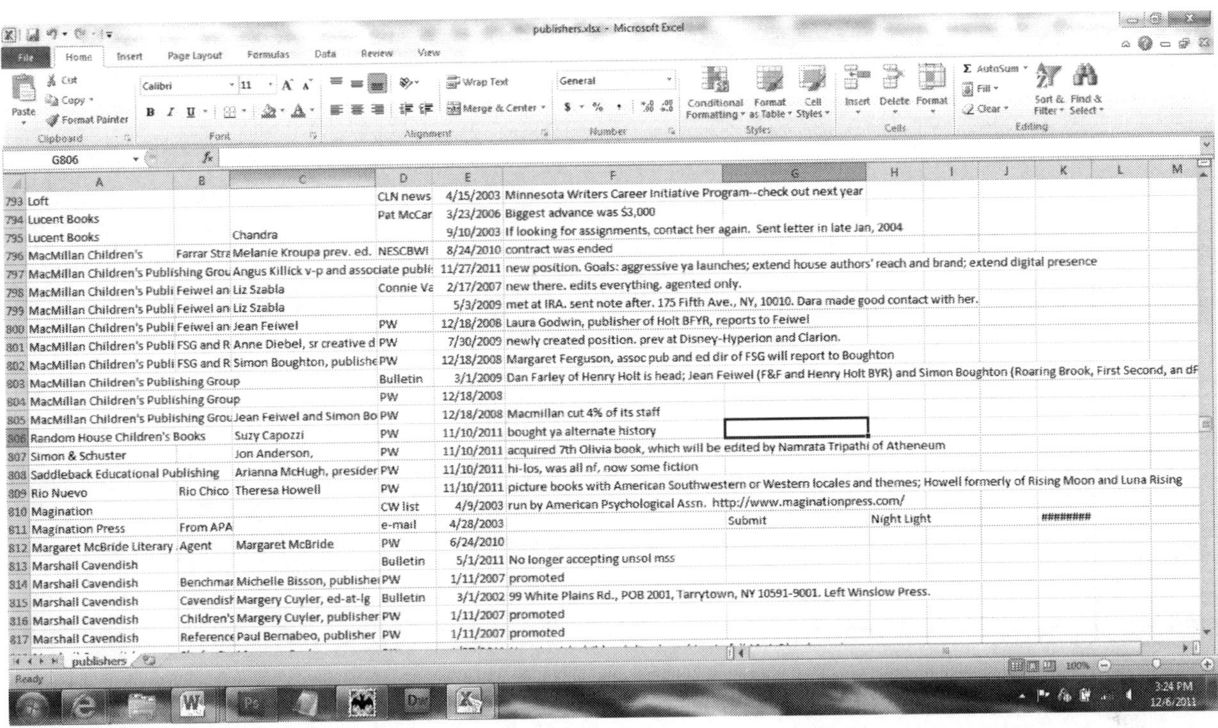

	A	B	C	D	E	F	G	H	I	J	K
793	Loft			CLN news	4/15/2003	Minnesota Writers Career Initiative Program--check out next year					
794	Lucent Books			Pat McCar	3/23/2006	Biggest advance was $3,000					
795	Lucent Books		Chandra		9/10/2003	If looking for assignments, contact her again. Sent letter in late Jan, 2004					
796	MacMillan Children's	Farrar Stra	Melanie Kroupa prev. ed.	NESCBWI	8/24/2010	contract was ended					
797	MacMillan Children's Publishing Grou		Angus Killick v-p and associate publi:		11/27/2011	new position. Goals: aggressive ya launches; extend house authors' reach and brand; extend digital presence					
798	MacMillan Children's Publi	Feiwel an	Liz Szabla	Connie Va	2/17/2007	new there. edits everything. agented only.					
799	MacMillan Children's Publi	Feiwel an	Liz Szabla		5/3/2009	met at IRA. sent note after. 175 Fifth Ave., NY, 10010. Dara made good contact with her.					
800	MacMillan Children's Publi	Feiwel an	Jean Feiwel	PW	12/18/2008	Laura Godwin, publisher of Holt BFYR, reports to Feiwel					
801	MacMillan Children's Publi	FSG and R	Anne Diebel, sr creative d	PW	7/30/2009	newly created position. prev at Disney-Hyperion and Clarion.					
802	MacMillan Children's Publi	FSG and R	Simon Boughton, publishe	PW	12/18/2008	Margaret Ferguson, assoc pub and ed dir of FSG will report to Boughton					
803	MacMillan Children's Publishing Group			Bulletin	3/1/2009	Dan Farley of Henry Holt is head; Jean Feiwel (F&F and Henry Holt BYR) and Simon Boughton (Roaring Brook, First Second, an dF					
804	MacMillan Children's Publishing Group			PW	12/18/2008						
805	MacMillan Children's Publishing Grou		Jean Feiwel and Simon Bo	PW	12/18/2008	Macmillan cut 4% of its staff					
806	Random House Children's Books		Suzy Capozzi	PW	11/10/2011	bought ya alternate history					
807	Simon & Schuster		Jon Anderson,	PW	11/10/2011	acquired 7th Olivia book, which will be edited by Namrata Tripathi of Atheneum					
808	Saddleback Educational Publishing		Arianna McHugh, presider	PW	11/10/2011	hi-los, was all nf, now some fiction					
809	Rio Nuevo	Rio Chico	Theresa Howell	PW	11/10/2011	picture books with American Southwestern or Western locales and themes; Howell formerly of Rising Moon and Luna Rising					
810	Magination			CW list	4/9/2003	run by American Psychological Assn. http://www.maginationpress.com/					
811	Magination Press	From APA		e-mail	4/28/2003		Submit	Night Light			########
812	Margaret McBride Literary	Agent	Margaret McBride	PW	6/24/2010						
813	Marshall Cavendish			Bulletin	5/1/2011	No longer accepting unsol mss					
814	Marshall Cavendish	Benchmar	Michelle Bisson, publishe	PW	1/11/2007	promoted					
815	Marshall Cavendish	Cavendist	Margery Cuyler, ed-at-lg	Bulletin	3/1/2002	99 White Plains Rd., POB 2001, Tarrytown, NY 10591-9001. Left Winslow Press.					
816	Marshall Cavendish	Children's	Margery Cuyler, publisher	PW	1/11/2007	promoted					
817	Marshall Cavendish	Reference	Paul Bernabeo, publisher	PW	1/11/2007	promoted					

The headings, in case you're wondering, are Publisher, Imprint, Editor, Source (where I got this info from), Date, Note, Action (what my next step should be), Manuscript 1 (what project I have that might be a good fit for this publisher), Manuscript 2, Manuscript 3, and Deadline (for me to take my next step).

And when I was first starting out writing for the educational market, I kept all my catalog and publisher analysis forms in one binder, and any info I heard about one of those publishers, I jotted down on the form.

Again, there's no right or wrong way to keep track. Do whatever you think you will really be able to maintain and use. And after you work at this market for six months or a year, you might find you need to track different info or you want to change the format you're tracking in. Go for it!

Lesson Nine

Writing Clips or Samples

Your introductory packet will likely include samples of your writing. A clip traditionally refers to a published piece, like a magazine article, that has been "clipped" from its published form (i.e., torn out of the magazine). A sample could be a published or unpublished piece of writing. If you have numerous children's books published, you might not have to send samples. Or you might. I still get asked for them sometimes.

Anyway, writing samples is a part of the introductory packet that overwhelms many writers. But it doesn't have to.

The rules are pretty simple.

- Send writing <u>for children</u>
- Send <u>nonfiction</u> writing
- <u>Identify on the page what the sample is</u> (for example, "Beginning of a magazine article aimed at 3rd to 5th graders" or "Introduction to book for 7th graders")

You can send more than one sample. Let's say you have one published piece of writing, and it's an article in a newsletter for adults. You can send that as one sample, as long as you **also** send one or two samples of nonfiction writing for kids.

Or, let's say you have had several short stories for kids published. Great! Again, you could include one, if you like, to "prove" your published status. But you should definitely send at least one nonfiction sample, as well.

What if you don't have any published nonfiction for kids? That's very common, and it's not a problem. You'll just write one!

HOMEWORK

Your homework is to examine your existing writing and determine whether or not you have any already-written pieces you can use for your writing samples.

Do you have any articles or nonfiction book manuscripts that you've written and had critiqued and revised and polished until they are in the best shape possible? If you do, great! You will just use one or more of those (or short excerpts from them) as your writing sample(s).

If you don't have any, then you'll start from scratch. Examine your topics list from earlier in the class and pick a couple of topics and age ranges (they can both be for the same age, if that's the age you really want to write for) to use for your writing samples. You don't have to take it any further yet—just pick your topics.

Lesson Ten

Writing Samples from Scratch

Your homework for lesson nine was to look for a sample among your already written works. But don't beat yourself up if you don't have a published clip or an appropriate writing sample to send. The solution is to simply write a sample from scratch.

THE STEPS FOR CREATING A WRITING SAMPLE

First, choose a topic you would like to write about. Remember, the writing sample you submit does **not** dictate the topic of the assignment you might get! So just because you create a writing sample about hydraulic engines does not commit you to writing an entire book about them! Look at the topics list you created for Lesson Four to get ideas for your writing sample.

Second, choose the age you are going to write for. What grade student might be interested in this topic? At what age in school do they study this topic? How much research do you want to do for this writing sample? What age kids do you feel comfortable writing for?

The audience age you choose for this sample is important. If you send two samples for primary grades, the editor is most likely going to consider you **only** for an assignment for that age range. So put some thought into the audience age. And if you are open to writing for various ages, perhaps send one sample for teens and another for 2nd graders, or something like that.

Third, choose the form you are going to write in. Are you going to write a nonfiction article? Are you going to write the introduction or part of chapter one of a book? Make sure you are clear about what you're writing. You will also include this info on your actual sample.

HOW LONG SHOULD THE SAMPLE BE?

Each sample can be just a couple of typed pages…about 500 words. You don't have to write a complete article (although if it's for very young kids, it might be complete at 500 words) or book. You're just showcasing your ability to put together interesting sentences, share facts, and identify appropriate audiences for your writing.

For instance, if you submit 500 words that you identify as the beginning of a magazine article for 1st graders, and it's clear that you're barely getting into the topic by the end of those 500 words, that isn't good. It shows that you don't realize that texts (even articles) for this age are very, very short. But if it's the beginning of a book for 5th graders, 500 words might well be just the opening anecdote.

IF YOU'RE TOTALLY LOST

If you have no idea where to start, here's a suggestion. From your library, check out several books from one series you like from the publisher you're approaching. Come up with a subtopic that would fit that series. If it's a series about construction machines and they don't have a book on tower cranes, pretend you have an assignment to write about tower cranes in the same style as that series. Now, write the first 500 words of the book. Match the tone and style and the amount of content covered in the first 500 words of the other books in that series.

I don't recommend doing this for every publisher! Once you have a good sample or two, use them with every introductory packet. This is just a place to get started for that very first one, that's all!

A SAMPLE SAMPLE

Here's a sample I wrote from scratch. Steck-Vaughn, an educational publisher, wanted people to write for a new series, and they asked for samples that were casual in tone and for a preteen/teen level. I had nothing appropriate to submit, so I wrote this article. (Steck-Vaughn was interested in hiring me to write, but the whole project fell through. On the plus side, I finished the article and sold it to *Girls Life* magazine!)

Laura Purdie Salas
10000 Main Street
Minneapolis, MN 55400
lpsalas@gmail.com
Unpublished first half of a preteen/teen magazine article **[Always include this kind of identification!]**
587 words

Helping Your Parents Say Yes

You already know your parents can say no. Can a friend spend the night? No. Will they buy you a car when you turn 16? No.

No problem. You might be surprised to learn that parents want to say yes. They want to do things for you. They want you to have fun. This is true.

So why do they say no so often? And how can you get them to say yes?

Let's say your friend Katy has invited you to spend Spring Break with her family. They have a condo in Florida. You can spend the whole week at the beach. You really want to do this. Really.

There is a right way and a wrong way to ask your parents for permission. Here's one way.

Mom walks in the door carrying groceries.

You say, "Mom, can I go to the beach for a week with Katy?"

"What?"

"The beach, Mom. For a whole week. Come on," you whine. You hop up and down with impatience. "Please?"

"I don't even know what you're talking about," says Mom.

"Come on. Just say yes. Please?" you say.

Mom gets more bags of food from the car. You stand there. "Please?"

Mom drops the bags on the counter. "Forget it," she says.

OK, that was the wrong way. Follow these steps for the best way to ask your parents for permission.

Step 1: Before you ask

Your mom and dad have probably said no lots of times. Think back to some of those conversations. Why did they say no? Was it money? Driving time? Interfering with the family schedule? Fear of misbehavior?

Figure out why they might say no this time. Make a list. Think like your parents. Try to come up with every objection they will. You might think the reasons are dumb. Write them down anyway.

Next, come up with an answer for every objection. Maybe your mom will say, "It's too expensive." Be ready to answer that. Tell her that Katy's family will be providing the housing and food. All you need is spending money.

Also, be willing to explain why you want to go. Tired parents might ask, "What's the big deal?" You have to be able to explain why this event is important to you. Here's a hint. Don't say that everyone else is going somewhere for Spring Break. Maybe they are. That doesn't matter. Don't say it. Try, "I'd love to visit the ocean." Or, "I haven't spent much time with Katy lately."

Step 2: Asking

Choose the right time to ask for permission. Let your parents know you want to ask them something. Agree on a time to chat. Don't ask them when anyone is rushed. Don't ask in the car. Don't ask right as they're getting home from work. Choose a quiet time to sit down together.

Be respectful. If you talk politely, the conversation will go much better. Maybe you and your parents argue a lot. It can be hard to break that habit. Pretend you are talking with your favorite teacher.

Ask your parents not to decide right away. You're eager for an answer. But your parents might need time to think about your request. Don't push them to answer right away. The answer will probably be no.

Be realistic. Are your parents going to let you miss six weeks of school to go on a two million dollar tour of Europe? Probably not. Don't keep asking for completely unrealistic things. It will annoy your mom and dad.

Your samples should always have your name and page number on each page, and I would also put in your email or phone number. Make it as easy as possible for the editor to contact you, even if all she has is your writing sample.

HOMEWORK

Your homework is to write a sample from scratch if you do not already have at least one nonfiction sample to send with your introductory packets. If you have one sample, but would like to create a second one (which I would recommend), then do that. If you already have two or more, you're off the hook (other than formatting them and including info on the kind of manuscript it is). This is not a one-night assignment. Remember, this is an audition of sorts, so you want to do a great job. Research interesting facts, write clearly, and present your work professionally.

FAQ

1) *Should I double-space or single-space my writing samples?*

If it's a published piece, you simply photocopy it and send it in. If it's unpublished, or if it's published but the submission guidelines ask for unedited manuscripts, then the general rule is that you should double-space. You could probably get by with 1.5 spacing if it would keep it to one page.

2) *Where do I identify what kind of writing sample it is?*

I make the information about what the piece is (unpublished writing sample: magazine article for 3rd graders) prominent. I just place it below my contact info in the upper left corner of the first page. The tone of a 500-word book about dogs for 1st graders has a totally different feel than a 500-word magazine article excerpt for 7th graders. If an editor doesn't know WHAT your manuscript is, she won't be able to evaluate your writing skills.

3) *For a published clip, what if the name of the magazine or newspaper is not on the page?*

If the magazine/book name and date isn't already on that page, I hand write it with a marker on the page.

Lesson Eleven

Proposals

> ***Attention***! You might not ever need to write a proposal. If you are open to assignments on a variety of topics, and if you plan to write for elementary school kids, you can ignore this chapter. If you find you are asked to write a proposal in the future, you can always come back to it. But a proposal is NOT part of the standard introductory packet, so don't worry about this information unless you have reason to think you'll be writing a proposal soon.

If you're interested in writing for secondary students, a publisher may request a proposal before giving you a contract for a book, even if the publisher chooses the subject. Even books for upper elementary kids occasionally start with a proposal.

The other time you might need a proposal is when you want to propose a book or series on a topic you're interested in.

So, I'm sharing a little information here. But if you simply offer your writing services to various educational publishers, you do **NOT** need to worry about a proposal right now. So skip this lesson and come back if you need it later.

There are a few different times/ways you might write a proposal.

ONE-PAGE SERIES PROPROSAL

First, perhaps you want to propose a series idea. What I would start out with is simply a one-page brief proposal. Here's one I wrote, and the publisher passed on it. I still might refine and polish it more.

Series Proposal: Body Talk (for grades 1-3)

Titles
Fitness: Make Me Strong
Nutrition: Feed Me Right
Sleep: Give Me a Break
Feelings: Let Them Out
Safety: Take Care of Me
Illnesses: Keep Me Healthy

Premise

A body would narrate each book, talking to the reader as if it is the reader's own body. I picture a different body and voice for each book, allowing a good mix of gender and ethnicity for the characters. I would use humor and kid language to acknowledge that good nutrition or plenty of sleep isn't always easy or fun. But I'll show why it's important to take care of your body and your mind and emphasize how powerful kids can be when it comes to self-care.

Educational Standards

This series would be aligned with the standards "Physical Health" and "Mental Health" as required by Benchmarks for Science Literacy: Project 2061.

Text Excerpt (from Nutrition: Feed Me Right)

Hey you! Yes, you. It's me, your body. Now, you might think that the best diet is ice cream, bologna, and chicken strips kid's meals. But you know what? I can't take too much of that stuff.

I know, I know. You like it, right? So does your mouth. Uh huh, your taste buds just go wild every time you eat a candy bar.

Just one problem. After that junk food leaves your mouth, the rest of your body has to put up with it. And that's not much fun.

Now one candy bar isn't going to hurt you. You know that. The problem really starts when you eat too much junk food and not enough nutritional food. That can affect lots of different parts of me and you.

Let's start with the bones. You know what they are, right? Those hard white things that form your skeleton. They hold you up and protect your organs. Well, bones need plenty of calcium to grow thick and strong.

How do you get that calcium? For one thing, you put down the grape soda and drink some milk. And when your daddy puts broccoli on your plate, go ahead and eat it. Greens and beans are the best way to get calcium that your bones can absorb easily. So chow down on those green beans and Brussels sprouts.

PROPOSAL FOR A NEW TITLE IN AN EXISTING SERIES

Second, maybe you want to propose a book for an existing series. To do that, you would simply say in your cover letter that you enjoy their series, XYZ. Then you ask if they would be interested in having you write a book on Topic B to fit into that series. That paragraph might look something like this.

"I especially enjoyed your Coming to America series. I would love to write a book for this series, perhaps one featuring a teenager from Ethiopia or Russia. Would you be interested in seeing a proposal for a book for this series? Otherwise, I'm open to assignments for books for any of your upper elementary series."

At that point, the editor might ask you for a proposal, and you would proceed from there.

PROPOSAL ON A TOPIC REQUESTED BY THE PUBLISHER

Or, related to this, **maybe the publisher asks you to write a proposal for a book on some other certain topic**.

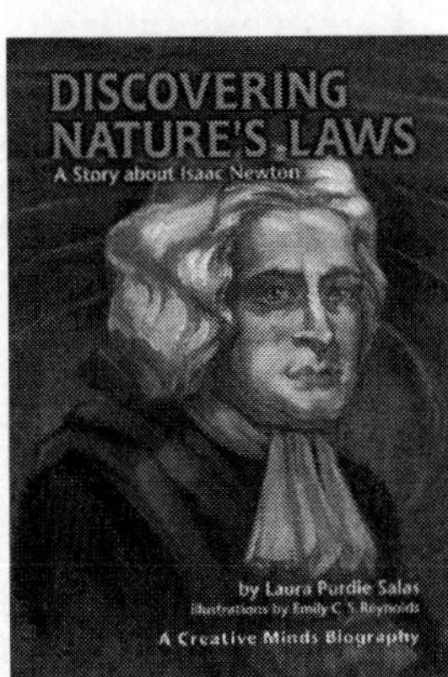

In either case, you ask what components they would like your proposal to include. An editor at Lerner asked if I wanted to do a biography. She gave me some people to choose from, and I chose Isaac Newton. I read a bunch of books from the same line of biographies (the Creative Minds series) to get a good understanding of how they were structured. Then I did a chapter summary outline and a cover letter to both express my enthusiasm for the topic, and also to give the editor a heads-up about some of my concerns about the proposed book (to cover myself in case I ran into serious problems later). I wrote the first chapter and created a bibliography showing the resources I had so far tracked down.

I didn't need to talk about what standards the book met or anything about marketing, etc. When it's a series the publisher is already publishing, they've already done all that work!

Here's an example of this kind of proposal.

Laura Purdie Salas
123 Main St. * Anytown, MN 55829
555-555-5555 * lpsalas@email.net
www. Laurasalas.com

Jill Braithwaite, Senior Editor
Lerner Publishing Group
241 First Avenue North
Minneapolis, MN 55401

Day/Month/Year

Dear Jill:

Well, here's my proposal on Isaac Newton for the On My Own series. I've included chapter one, a chapter outline, and a bibliography.

Isaac Newton was a fascinating man, full of contradictions. He was part medieval, part modern. A mathematician and magician. He accomplished great things in his life, but he was not well liked by many people. He wanted people to admire his discoveries, but he did not like to publish his findings. He was willing to help other scientists when he wasn't feuding with them. He lived a lonely life much of the time, although he had periods of sociability. He had periods of mental illness, which some scholars believe is manic depressive disorder and others think is mercury poisoning. In addition to his scientific studies, he spent a lot of time on alchemy and Bible interpretation. This man of science believed in literal interpretation of the Bible. In short, he was a real person, not just the guy with the apple.

There are some things that set Newton apart from Most of the other biography subjects in your series. He was not entirely likeable, for one. And because he lived so long ago, specific details on some incidents are hard to come by. He did not keep a diary or publish an autobiography, as many of the subjects did. He had a variety of interests, even obsessions, so there is not really a focus on one accomplishment or discovery. The contradictions of his life form a theme of the book. I think his complexity and his amazing scientific contributions make him an excellent biography subject.

His childhood, covered in chapter one, is the least documented portion of his life. As an adult, he was a prolific letter writer, so future chapters will include quotes to show the flavor of his personality. And he did have a couple of close friends in his life who wrote about him, and those manuscripts, based on the excerpts I've read, should provide further insight.

I look forward to hearing your reaction to the sample chapter. Thanks for this opportunity, and I hope you're enjoying the holiday season.

Sincerely,
Laura Purdie Salas

Chapter Outline

1 – **Fire in the Sky** – Isaac Newton had a difficult childhood. His father died before Isaac was born in 1642, and he spent little time with his mother. When he went away to school at age 11, he was placed in the lowest class. After a schoolyard fight, Isaac began concentrating on his studies. He was soon a top student. In his teenage years, Isaac built strange, clever models, like a miniature windmill run by a mouse and a kite that carried a flame. Although he was considered a genius by his teen years, he was not good at making friends. When Isaac was 17, his mother called him home to manage the family farm.

2 – **Not Fit for Farming** – Isaac spent two disastrous years at Woolsthorpe, his family's farm estate. A servant tried to teach Isaac how to run the farm, but Isaac was not a good student. While he was supposed to be tending sheep, he would build dams and models and let the sheep ramble onto neighboring property. When the servant went to town to buy supplies, Isaac would bribe him to go alone so he could read and study. Finally, to the relief of the servants, who said he was "fit for nothing but the 'Versity," Isaac's mother agreed to let him return to school to prepare for Cambridge University. His first few years at Cambridge studying physics and mathematics were uneventful.

3 – **The Miracle Years** – In 1665, Cambridge University closed because of the plague. Isaac returned to Woolsthorpe for two years, known as the Miracle Years. In that time, Isaac studied and experimented and came up with the basics of his biggest contributions to science. During this time, the falling apple sparked ideas about how gravity worked.

4 – **The Principia** – Isaac returned to Cambridge University and became a professor. His teachings were beyond the grasp of Most students, and he often lectured to empty halls. He built a reflecting telescope, which was much smaller but more powerful and accurate than existing telescopes. This device gained him an invitation to the Royal Society of London, an intellectual group. He stayed at Cambridge for 20 years, during which he wrote many papers on the nature of light and color. He also studied alchemy and the Bible. He published his Most famous work, known now as the Principia, in 1687. This is still considered one of the Most important scientific papers ever written, and it was published in three books. It included Isaac's three laws of motions and his law of gravity.

5 – **Illness and Arguments** – After publishing Principia, Isaac spent less time on his studies. He served in Parliament for one year and then in 1693 suffered some illness in which he turned against his friends. Some scientists today believe he had mercury poisoning. Many feel he was mentally ill. Isaac, who had a long history of disputes with other scientists, was also involved in a long argument over the invention of calculus.

6 – **Master of the Mint** – Isaac spent the last 30 years of his life working for the government Mint at the Tower of London. Even though the position was meant to be just a formality, Isaac got very involved in the actual running of the Mint. He tracked down counterfeiters and helped decide on the designs of new coins. He became involved in academic circles again and was elected president of the Royal Society. He was the first person to be knighted for contributions to science. Isaac died at the age of 84.

Afterword – How have Isaac Newton's laws and theories stood up over three-and-a-half centuries? How do they affect us today?

Chapter One--Fire in the Sky

Isaac Newton had an idea. He would play a trick on the people of his town. First, he made a kite. Isaac loved to make kites. He had figured out the best shape for a kite and the best spot to attach the strings.

Then he got out the folded paper lantern he had made. Isaac used it to light his way to school on winter mornings. When he got to school, he always put out the flame, folded up the lantern, and stored it in his pocket.

But now twelve-year-old Isaac had a better use for his lantern. That night, he lit the lantern and attached it to the kite. He stood in an open windy field and sailed the kite into the dark English sky.

The flame danced and flickered in the air. It terrified the people of Grantham. In England in the 1650s, people were not used to seeing moving lights in the sky.

When market day came, the townspeople drank mugs of ale and discussed the mysterious light. Nobody guessed that Isaac had anything to do with it. Many people thought the flashing light was a comet, but it wasn't. It was just another of Isaac Newton's bright ideas.

Isaac was born in 1642 at Woolsthorpe Manor, his family's country estate. He was born prematurely on Christmas Day. He was so tiny he could have fit into a one-quart milk jug. Nobody thought Isaac would survive. In fact, when two women walked to a neighbor's house for his medicine, they sat and chatted on a fence. They were so sure he would die that they didn't hurry.

[I included the entire first chapter...this is just the beginning of it.]

SOURCE LIST

The bold sources are the ones that I quoted directly. I also put asterisks by the most helpful sources. *[Note: This is the first page of my bibliography.]*

*Anderson, Margaret J. Isaac Newton: The Greatest Scientist of All Time. Springfield: Enslow Publishers, Inc., 1996.

Andrade, Edward Neville de Costa. Sir Isaac Newton [his life and work]. Garden City, NY: Anchor Books, Doubleday & Company, Inc.: 1954.

Berlinski, David. Newton's Gift: How Sir Isaac Newton Unlocked the System of the World. Simon & Schuster, 2000.

Broad, William J. "Sir Isaac Newton: Mad as a Hatter," Science, September 18, 1981, pp. 1341+.

Buchdahl, Gerd. The Image of Newton and Locke in the Age of Reason. Sheed and Ward, 1961.

Carrell, Jennifer Lee. "Newton's vice: Some say alchemy inspired our greatest scientist," Smithsonian, December 2000, pp. 130+.

Cohen, I. Bernard. "Newton's Discovery of Gravity," Scientific American, March, 1981, pp. 167+.

Craig, Sir John. "Isaac Newton and the Counterfeiters." Notes and Records of the Royal Society, 18 (1963), 136–145.

Craig, John Herbert. Newton at the Mint. Cambridge University Press, 1946.

De Morgan, Augustus. Newton: His Friend: And His Niece. London: Elliot Stock, 1885.

Falk, Dan. "The Genius of Woolsthorpe," British Heritage, June 1999, pp.20+.

Gardner, Martin. "Isaac Newton: alchemist and fundamentalist," Skeptical Inquirer, Sep–Oct, 1996, pp. 13+.

Hall, A. Rupert. Isaac Newton: Adventurer in Thought. Cambridge: Blackwell Publishers, 1992.

TRADE NONFICTION PROPOSALS

Third, and this is really outside the scope of this workbook, but most trade publishers and a few small educational publishers expect a much more detailed proposal. This is really a trade nonfiction proposal. I'm including a sample here, though, because perhaps you want to write for the trade nonfiction market as well and might find this useful. Or if an educational publisher asked for a detailed proposal, you might include some of these components as well.

The sample I'm going to share here is for a book I really wanted to write. So I did an in-depth proposal and approached a few niche market trade publishers. So, this was not a proposal assigned to me.

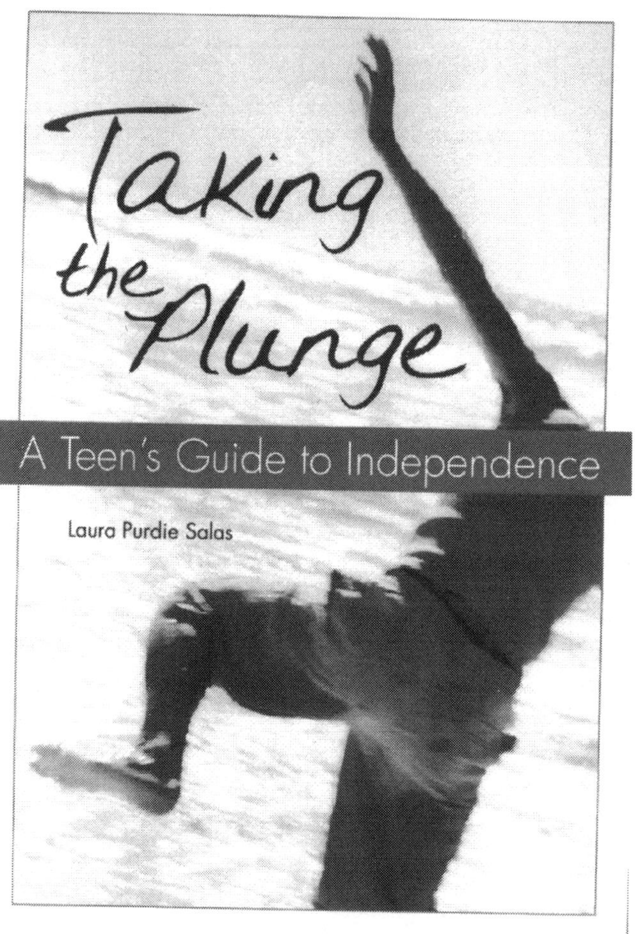

Taking the Plunge: A Teen's Guide to Independence

by

Laura Purdie Salas

Laura Purdie Salas
123 Main Street
Minneapolis, MN 55488
555-555-5555
laura@laura.net

About the Author

Laura Purdie Salas is a children's writer and the author of 10 nonfiction books for kids. She has written 8 books for Capstone Press: **Forest Fires** (hi-lo, 2001), **China** (hi-lo, 2001), **Germany** (hi-lo, 2001), **Ice Fishing** (hi-lo, 2002), **Canoeing** (hi-lo, 2002), **Snowmobiling** (hi-lo, 2002), **Trail of Tears** (2002), and **Wilderness Road** (2002). Steck-Vaughn just published her hi-lo book about skateboarding, called **The Thrill of the Ride**, as part of its new Power Up! Building Reading Strength program, and her biography of Isaac Newton will be coming out with Lerner Publishing in 2003.

Ms. Salas has also had her short fiction and poetry published in *New Moon, Turtle, Chickadee, The Friend*, story anthologies, and testing materials.

The topic of teen independence is one that Ms. Salas has wanted to write about for many years. One of four daughters of parents who didn't like children much, she started dreaming of living on her own at the age of 13. Her older sisters all married young to get out of the house, but she wanted to do it on her own terms. At the age of 16, she moved out of her parents' home and in with one of her sisters. Six months later, she moved into her own apartment and spent the next four years working full-time and going to college full-time. She looked for practical information on jobs, transportation, housing, and all the other topics that together build a smooth-running life. There was nothing aimed at teens, however. She scrounged around for the information, relying on her sisters, her guidance counselor, and trial-and-error to figure out the best way to accomplish her independence.

Now Ms. Salas would like to write the book she wishes she could have found 20 years ago. She wants to write a book that will help guide kids through the challenging job of creating an independent life while they're still teenagers.

Ms. Salas lives in Minnesota with her husband and two daughters. During her free time, she reads voraciously, does household projects, and spends time at her daughters' school.

About the Book

Kids grow up hearing “You’re not old enough.” Not old enough to drive, not old enough to work, not old enough to make their own decisions. But some teens, by choice or necessity, are living on their own. **Taking the Plunge: A Teen’s Guide to Independence** doesn’t tell teens they aren’t old enough. Instead, it shows them how to build a successful independent life, step by step.

Taking the Plunge is a workbook for teens filled with completely practical information: no preaching, no disapproving. For all the teens dreaming about moving out of the house, **Taking the Plunge** will show them the reality of independence, both its demands and rewards. It will help them decide whether they have the skills and determination to live independently. And if they decide they do, **Taking the Plunge** will be their guide.

The book will incorporate many features to make the material easier to understand and more visually appealing. By the Numbers boxes will highlight statistics related to the chapter’s topic. Work It Out pages will offer quizzes or worksheets for the reader to complete. How To sections will teach a skill to teens step-by-step, like How to balance a checkbook in chapter eight. The Ten Best sections will round up ten top ideas related to the chapter, like The ten best resources for paying for school in chapter four. Sidebars will present any other useful information that doesn’t fit into the flow of that chapter, and resource lists will point kids toward other books, web sites, and organizations to learn more about the chapter’s topic. Not every chapter will include every feature, but **Taking the Plunge** will contain enough variety to make the book simple to understand and satisfying to read.

The book is organized in a common-sense style, covering all the topics critical to independence. I will consult expert sources (government agencies, attorneys, social workers, field experts, research organizations) for each topic, giving teens the benefit of a book that’s easy to understand and is saturated with my enthusiasm for the topic, but that is informed by the latest information in every area.

Chapter Summaries

Chapter One: Take a Deep Breath: Before you dive into independence

Introduction to the book. Are you ready for true independence? A brief overview of what it means to be independent. Options for semi-independence.

By the Numbers: Teens on the street
Age minimums
Work It Out: Quiz: Are you ready for independence?
The Ten Best: Semi-independent living situations

Chapter Two: Climbing the Ladder: Using goals to reach your dreams

Setting goals for your life. Why you need goals when you leave home. Tips for vocational testing and financial planning. When, where, and how much to tell your parents about your plans.

By the Numbers: How many teens return home after moving out
Work It Out: Worksheet: Where do I want to be...?
How To: Tell your parents you're moving out
The Ten Best: Steps to prepare for independence
Sidebars: How to make your dreams come true
Resources: Motivational and goal-setting resources

Chapter Three: Your Coaching Team: Finding the people who will support you

If you're independent, why do you need help? Who can help you? Teachers, social workers, friends, and hopefully some of your relatives. Resources you can turn to if you're in a crisis.

By the Numbers: How many kids call crisis hotlines
Work It Out: Worksheet: Who's my support team?
How To: Ask for help
The Ten Best: Possibilities for your support team
Sidebars: When your parents are angry
Resources: Government agencies that can help you
Crisis agencies and hotlines

Chapter Four: Years of Practice: Does school train you for real life?

Dropping out vs. toughing it out. The GED. Job-training programs. How can you afford college if you're broke? SAT. Student loans.

By the Numbers: Avg. salaries of dropouts vs. high school grads vs. college grads
Work It Out:Quiz: Do you need to stay in school?
How To: Navigate the financial aid maze
The Ten Best: Resources for paying for school
Sidebars: Community college vs. a four-year college
Resources: Student loan info
ROTC
GED and SAT study aids

Chapter Five: Going Pro: Choosing the right job or career

Flipping burgers: Fine for a few years, but for the rest of your life? Career counseling. What kind of job do you want? Job-hunting. Interviewing skills. How to keep your job.

By the Numbers: Average pay for typical teen jobs
Work It Out: Worksheet: Job-interest inventory
How To: Write a resume
The Ten Best: Jobs you can get with one year of post-high-school training
Sidebars: Phony ads and job scams
Resources: Career book/web site?

Appendices: List of state departments of motor vehicles
List of state departments of education
List of state departments of labor

(Actual proposal included chapter summaries for the entire book)

About the Reader

Who will read this book? First and foremost, teens will be the readers of this book. Potential groups of kids who will be the audience for **Taking the Plunge** include:

- Kids living in abusive family situations
- Kids who crave independence for any number of reasons
- Kids whose families are homeless
- Kids whose parents are kicking them out of the house
- Kids already living on their own
- Kids who just think being on their own would be easier and more fun

Although the book is aimed primarily at teens, some adults will find the book useful to read in order to help teens who are trying to achieve independence. These groups of potential readers include:

- School guidance counselors
- Parents
- Older siblings
- Social workers
- Crisis line staff
- Homeless shelter staff
- Teachers of daily living skills
- Social justice professionals

I have thought about making this more of a general-interest book for all teens who are about to be independent for the first time, including kids going away to college, getting married, or simply moving out, but not due to a bad home life. I'm still open to that possibility, although for the time being I'm focusing on writing it as a guide for teens who might otherwise end up living on (or already are on) the streets.

About the Market

I'm disappointed to see that there are no more helpful books on this topic available today for teens than there were in 1983 when I became independent. I looked at the many, many books available on the topic of teens and homelessness and independence. All of them, with one exception, are written for social workers, parents, or professionals who work with teens. They are often in dry, academic prose and tend to be very theoretical.

The only practical handbook on this topic is called **Independence: A Lifeskills Guide for Teens**, published by the Child Welfare League of America in 1990. The problem is that it's outdated and all the resources listed are Canadian.

Even the book by Ellen Switzer called **Anyplace but Here: Young, alone, and homeless: What to do** (Atheneum, 1992) is not a how-to book, despite the title. It does not talk directly to teens, but instead describes some teens and their particular situations.

When we come across kids facing hard times at school, at work, through our friends, or on the street, we usually pass on by. If we are struck with compassion, we might talk to their parents, a teacher, or a social worker for advice. Rarely do we talk to the teens themselves to give them helpful information so that they can accomplish their goals. The same is true with the available books on topic. Books on teenage independence either talk to other adults about the problem or are more general books like **Life Strategies for Teens** (Fireside, 2000) and **What Teens Need to Succeed** (Free Spirit, 1998).

So, while the reading and using market for my book would be all teens who crave independence, the buying market is another matter.

I think the best way to get this book into the hands of its intended audience is to sell this book to social workers, teachers, school guidance counselors, psychologists, parents, and staff at homeless shelters and runaway shelters. Here are some possible markets for mailings or e-mailings about **Taking the Plunge**.

- American School Counselor Association
- National Runaway Switchboard
- National Coalition for the Homeless
- Child Welfare League of America
- State Departments of Family & Children's Services

I have a few other ideas about marketing this book as well.

I would look for teen magazine markets to write short pieces for (or to offer book excerpts to) on related topics. For example, perhaps *Careers & Colleges* would run a piece on college financing for the independent minor, and maybe *College Bound Magazine* would like an article on health issues for college kids. The blurb at the end of each article would identify **Taking the Plunge** as an upcoming book on teen independence.

I would also approach adult magazines/newsletters whose readers include **Taking the Plunge**'s target buying audience. *ASCA School Counselor* might be interested in an article on the practical advice guidance counselors can give teens who want to move out and quit school.

Another tool I'd be interested in using is the Internet. I would be willing to be responsible for maintaining a web site that has links to all the resources listed in the book plus more. I could include some printable worksheets (different from the ones in **Taking the Plunge**) and possibly a short new article each month on a topic relating to teen independence. I could offer extending activities for social workers and guidance counselors and other adults. A link from the web site could take viewers directly to Amazon or to your web site to purchase the book.

I'd also be willing to talk to teens at schools or shelters, telling my story and giving some basic advice. And I could talk to professionals at various conferences, explaining what it's like to be independent as a teen and what teens most need from those who want to help.

-END-

MORE ABOUT PROPOSALS

Here's a handout from a workshop I did on nonfiction proposals at SCBWI in L.A.

How to Write a Nonfiction Proposal

Purpose - To interest an editor in a book (prove there's a market) and show the editor you can write it

Types

Trade Market - A proposal for a standalone book that you determine everything for—scope, age of audience, format, tone, etc.

Educational Market - For a book in a series, and you follow the publisher's format, voice, age of audience, reading level, etc.

When Do You Write a Proposal?

You must fully understand the idea and be able to fully visualize your book before you write a proposal.

Trade Market - You can send a query and offer a complete proposal, or you can just submit a proposal straightaway

Educational Market - Often at editor's invitation on topic editor provides; sometimes to suggest a new series; to suggest a new title in an existing series

What Do You Include in a Proposal?

Trade Market

- Cover letter
    - Lead or hook
    - Persuasion/why is this important
    - Your biography/credentials (briefly)
    - Conclusion

- Title page - Includes all contact information
- About the Author
    - Make yourself sound as well-qualified as possible
    - Don't lie
    - Keep your credentials relevant to the book
    - Usually written in 3rd-person
    - Things to look for and use in this section:
        - Public speaking
        - Teaching
        - Certifications/licensure
        - Awards/recognition
        - Academic achievements/degrees/classes you've taken
        - Things written about you
        - Things written by you
        - Marketing/promotion efforts you've made
        - Writing that's been published

- About the Book
    - Describe the book in a compelling manner
    - What is the book's main point?
    - What is its size, length, and format?
    - Will it employ specific graphic elements?
    - Are photographs an issue? If so, can you provide them?
    - Where will you get information?

- Chapter Summaries
    - Reveals the structure of your book
    - Straightforward writing
    - Always in 3rd person

- The Market
  - Who will buy this book (especially important if your book is not part of an existing series): Age group, gender, ethnicity
  - Look beyond the obvious
  - Are there other buyers besides children for your book?
  - Use statistics to prove there's a market
  - List professional associations that might serve buyers
  - Any specialty venues? A field guide for young birdwatchers could be sold in national and state parks as well as bird supply stores
  - DON'T mention your own friends and family
  - DON'T exaggerate (your children's book won't land you on Oprah)

- The Competition
  - Use amazon.com to find titles
  - Don't use books that are out-of-print, self-published, or academic books in this list
  - List with title, author, publisher, and year
  - Tell briefly what each book does and what it fails to do (be factual, not rude)
  - Make a statement about why your book will be better and different than all these competing titles.

- Promotion
  - What will you do to help sell your book?
  - Start with Most impressive things
  - Some of these may tie in to your About the Author credentials. If you do school visits, for instance, that's a great platform for book sales.
  - How many book-related talks will you give each year?
  - Do you have contacts in the media?
  - Do you have a good hook for interviews?
  - Do you have a promotional budget? Will you spend your advance on promotion?
  - Do you have sales experience?
  - Will you hire a publicist?
  - Will you visit bookstores in major cities? How many?
  - Will you speak at conferences/conventions? Which ones? Where?
  - Will you give workshops at which you'll sell your book?
  - Be as specific as possible

Educational Market

- Cover letter
  - Thank her for opportunity
  - Sell her on book (even though they picked the topic)
  - Express concerns (as positively as possible)
  - Mention some sources

- Outline
  - Follow format of other books in series (I read about 11)
  - Keep to one page unless editor requests more detail

- Sample chapter
  - Make it match the rest of the series in vocabulary, tone, length, structure, subheads, etc.

What Not to Include in a Proposal

- Inappropriate submissions
- Gifts/bribes
- Copyright information

There are also numerous books out there on writing book proposals. They can give you more detailed information than I've shared here. Look for books that were published or updated within the past 3 years so that they reflect current industry practices.

To repeat, feel free to incorporate the offer of a proposal or the mention of a specific book into your cover letter IF IT'S SOMETHING YOU REALLY WANT TO DO. Otherwise, just stay more general and offer your services up for hire for whatever series the editors need writers for. That's how my cover letters have generally been, and it's the way you give the editor the most options. Also, keep in mind that you can propose a certain book or series but ALSO let the editor know that you're open to assignments on many different topics. You don't have to restrict yourself to one option or the other.

Lesson Twelve

Get Feedback on Your Cover Letter

Before you move on, you might need to tweak your cover letter. Now that you've decided what other components you will include in your introductory packet, you might need to mention some of them in your cover letter. For instance, perhaps you'll say, after sharing your topics of interest, that one of your writing samples is about one of those topics.

So, before going to the next step, look over your first draft of your cover letter and make any changes to it that you think are necessary.

The next step is having someone else critique your cover letter. You have several options here. If you already belong to a writing group, then you're all set, as long as your group has strong writers in it with experience in editorial correspondence. If you don't belong to such a group, you can hire a professional writer or editor to critique your letter. There are many options online—you're best off with someone who has some experience in the educational market, but any professional writer or editor should be able to give you helpful feedback. Through Mentors for Rent, Lisa Bullard (another writer who writes extensively for the educational market) and I also critique cover letters and/or introductory packets. You can learn more at www.MentorsForRent.com. Getting strong feedback will help you see how to revise your cover letter to make it even better.

TIPS FOR YOUR LETTER

Here are a few other tips I often find myself giving writers, so check your cover letter over for these issues before you send it out:

* Make sure you don't overwhelm with details. You do want to show how you're qualified to write for this company. But you don't want to overwhelm with too many details of your school and work experience. Share just the *very* best highlights and put the rest on your resume. This is especially important since writing for the ed market means cutting/editing your work to the bare bones on a regular basis. Your letter is the first evidence that you can do that!

* Ask a question near the end. You don't have to do this, but I like to close a letter asking the editor a definite question, like, "Do you have any assignments available?" or "Would you like to talk about possible assignments?" That is a small spur to action on the part of the editor.

* Keep your cover letter to **one** typewritten page (at LEAST 11 pt. type, PREFERABLY 12 pt.)

CRITIQUING CRITERIA

Now, here's what I focus on while critiquing cover letters. So if you're getting critiques from other writers, share this list with them when you give them the copy of your letter.

First, I do like to be encouraging! Share at least one sentence, phrase, or word that you think worked well.

Also, I look for the following things:

- Is it professionally written/formatted?
- Does the writer present herself in a professional, competent manner?
- Does she share her strong points as a possible writer for this company?
- Does she do the above without coming across as "too good" for the company?
- Does she say something to show the editor that she has some familiarity with the books the publisher publishes?
- Does her letter reflect enthusiasm at the possibility of working with the editor?
- Is there contact info included?

- Does the length feel right? (It should be one typed page at the most.)
- Is the letter free of typographical errors, and has the writer double-checked the name and spelling and title of the letter's recipient.

Writers, when your cover letter is critiqued, either by me or by someone else, please don't take it personally. The point of a critique is to help you improve. I get my writing critiqued regularly, and my writing is always stronger because of it. (Even if it occasionally stings a little bit at the moment:>)

HOMEWORK

Please send your cover letter to a trusted critique partner or to a professional critique/editor.

Lesson Thirteen

Analyzing a Series

In this lesson, we're talking about series, since educational publishers produce books almost exclusively in series. I'm hoping that by the end of this lesson, you'll understand better how precisely your writing needs to match the existing series. This part of the process is often a shock to a potential writer!

WHEN DO YOU ANALYZE A SERIES?

The ability to study a series is going to come in handy in several situations.

First, when you're studying publishers, you might look at some of their series so that you can mention how much you'd like to write for that particular series.

Second, if you're asked to write a proposal (this varies widely—I've only once been asked to write a proposal!), studying the series will show you how you need to structure your own book.

Third, if you want to do a brief proposal for a book that fits into a certain series, you can say things like, "Like the other books in the series, my book would be 48 pages and contain 6 chapters. I would include Read More and Glossary segments." Stuff like this shows the editor you've studied the series and are a professional. It will show that you realize your book must match the others in the series.

Fourth, when you actually have an assignment, studying the series will be helpful, too, though you'll also likely have series guidelines to help you.

So, now that I've convinced you it's important, how do you go about doing it? Easy!

Gather 4 to 6 books from the same series. Not just the same publisher, but the actual same series. For instance, here's a series.

https://www.lernerbooks.com/products/s/s21/LB/series
http://tinyurl.com/6uz43f4

Here's another.

http://rourkepublishing.com/series/223
http://tinyurl.com/87ursdv

This is a series.

http://www.marshallcavendish.us/marshallcavendish-us/benchmark/catalog/american_studies/Controversy!/index.xml
http://tinyurl.com/79cckg4

Basically, open any educational publisher's catalog, turn to a page, and you'll see a series!

So, gather your books, and look them over, and then fill in the form on the next page.

If you don't have access to four books in a series (for instance, if you're not in the U.S.), here's a substitute activity. You can look at these four brief videos of me showing four different series I worked on. Ugh—I hate seeing myself on camera, so I share these with trepidation! But I do want you to have an option, so here you go:

Series Analysis: Animals All Around
http://www.youtube.com/watch?v=WmtZlCQKA_I
http://tinyurl.com/2ef36r5

Series Analysis: Write Your Own
http://www.youtube.com/watch?v=PGXRdkv-3NE
http://tinyurl.com/23tkbsb

Series Analysis: Science Songs
http://www.youtube.com/watch?v=S0RPftQLZZg
http://tinyurl.com/22lnsm6

Series Analysis: ABC Books
http://www.youtube.com/watch?v=4HnApQpvOII
http://tinyurl.com/2bapx8g

You'll see how similar all the books are! (At least, this is true 99% of the time. No doubt at least one of you reading this book will find an exception, because that's the way things work!)

Series Analysis Form

Publisher: Series:

Age range:

Title	Wds	Pgs	Chs	Lead	POV	Tone	Extras	Misc

You'll note the title, how many words, how many pages, how many chapters, what style of lead (any introduction? anecdote? same kind of anecdote, like childhood story in a biography? jump right into chapter one?), point of view (standard second person? third person? first person?), tone (casual? formal? humorous?), extras (glossary? craft activities? word games?), and misc (miscellaneous--that's for anything else that strikes you as specific to this series).

HOMEWORK

Please fill out the Series Analysis form for one series. If, by chance, you got more than one series, analyze them all! You can make copies of the Series Analysis form—there's a blank form at the back of the book. One tip: To find the word counts for books, go the Renaissance Learning website.

http://www.renlearn.com/store/quiz_home.asp
http://tinyurl.com/y42sd4

Think about your results. Were you surprised at how similar the books in the series were? Do they make the task of writing this kind of book feel more daunting? Or less?

Also, work on your writing sample if you haven't finished that yet.

Lesson Fourteen

Series Guidelines

While you're waiting for feedback on your cover letter, we'll move on to talking about the actual assignments a little bit. First, I just want to reassure you that when you get an assignment to write a book, you will not just be thrown to the wolves! Ninety percent of the time, you will get series guidelines.

Series guidelines are a document written by a team of people at the publishing house. These guidelines usually serve several purposes. They show what the purpose of a series is, which curriculum standards the series will help teachers meet, what the titles in a series are, what the components of the series are (as far as extra elements, kind of illustration, etc.), etc.

The best way for me to explain series guidelines to you is to show some samples.

Excerpt One

DESCRIPTION: A series of reluctant reader books, each featuring one type of music that grew out of grass-roots cultural groups as opposed to big-name recording studios. Each book will include topical chapter text as well as snippets (as longer captions next to photos). High-interest action photos will show musicians, dancers, and fans creating and enjoying the music. Glossary words will also be defined at point of use in callout boxes throughout text.

INTEREST LEVEL: Grades 5-9 (Reluctant Reader)
READING LEVEL: Grade 4 Fry
FORMAT: 6½" X 9 ¼"
WORDS: 4,800-5,000 words (including snippets)
PAGES: 48
ILLUSTRATIONS: about 40-50 including a cover, color

PARTS: Title page, CIP, Table of Contents, Sidebars, Chapter Notes, Timeline, Glossary, Further Reading, Internet Addresses, Index

MARKETING POINTS:
1. High-interest topics encourage reading, help them develop good reading habits, and motivate them to continue reading in the future.
2. Lots of info. for report writers. Good storytelling to hold readers' interest.
3. Lively, inviting 4-C design and lots of action photos to attract readers.
4. Includes Timeline, Glossary, Further Reading and Internet Addresses.

AVAILABLE TITLES IN THE SERIES:
[NOTE: In each case, focus must be on the "bling," etc—FUN; not intellectual]
1. The Rap Scene: The People, the Image, the Music (note: rap is a subgenre of hip-hop)
...

BODY
(each numbered item below is a spread)
1. Hot Stuff—(today's latest and greatest, how the music is new and exciting, current famous artists, new technology)
2. "I'm Your Biggest Fan!" (who listens the music? ages, cultural groups, clothing/style, etc.)
3. Outfitted (clothing and accessory styles and how they have changed—definitely would be cool visually to show typical styles from the genre's beginnings versus today)
...Each spread should contain at least 2 photographs (in majority of spreads, this should include at least 1 of an artist)—very visual design. There would also be multiple fast facts, small sidebars, etc. throughout each book.

Excerpt Two

Type of book: Informational picture book
Written for ages/grades: Grades 2–3
Marketed to ages/grades: Ages 6–8; Grades 1–4

Objectives: To introduce readers to the animal and plant life cycles using appropriate vocabulary and examples. The reader will understand <u>that plants and animals progress through life cycles of birth, growth and development, reproduction, and death; the details of these life cycles are different for different organisms</u>

Key Words/Concepts and Individual Title Focus :

Plants
* Plants change their forms as part of their life cycles.
* The life cycles of flowering plants include seed germination, growth, flowering, pollination and seed dispersal.
* Describe the life cycles of flowering plants as they grow from seeds, proceed through maturation and produce new seeds.
* Explore and describe the effects of light and water on seed germination

Maple tree (MD, MA)
Daisy (FL)

Trim size: 10x10
Page count: 24 pages
Words per spread: (3–4 sentences—can be up to 5–6 if sentences are very short)
Number of spreads: 9
Illustration style: Similar to previous sets

Front Matter:
Title Page
CIP

Table of Contents: Chapters of varying lengths. Back matter entries indented or set off in some way to make for an easier distinction for primary reader

Features in Main Text:
Sidebars of interesting tidbits or related/supporting information (on Most spreads, not required on all—please keep sidebars to appropriate reading level)
horizontal timeline across spread to indicate where reader is.

Excerpt Two Continued:

Main Text:

Make the reader feel as if they have gained something in the reading that they didn't know before Provide 2 or 3 facts per spread

First spread should explain that there are several/many different kinds of deciduous trees or flowers or dogs or amphibians (whatever is appropriate) and that this book will focus on one

Use simple language but don't be simplistic

Alignment with Curriculum Standards:
State which mention organism specifically in their standards are indicated after each topic in the Individual Title List.
California Grade 2 Life Sciences
Plants and animals have predictable life cycles. As a basis for understanding this concept:
a. *Students know* that organisms reproduce offspring of their own kind and that the offspring resemble their parents and one another.
b. *Students know* the sequential stages of life cycles are different for different animals, such as butterflies, frogs, and mice.
c. *Students know* many characteristics of an organism are inherited from the parents. Some characteristics are caused or influenced by the environment.
d. *Students know* there is variation among individuals of one kind within a population.
e. *Students know* light, gravity, touch, or environmental stress can affect the germination, growth, and development of plants.
f. *Students know* flowers and fruits are associated with reproduction in plants.

Excerpt Three

SERIES TITLE: Write Your Own
Fall 07: Tall tales, poetry, biography, myths

OBJECTIVES:
Write Your Own reinforces that good writers are readers. It provides the distinguishing characteristics of each genre and uses examples from classic and popular age-appropriate books as instructional tools and models for the readers own writing. The series shows readers how to work within the common writing model to develop characters, plots, and settings, as well as satisfying beginnings, middles, and endings. Most common process used: prewriting, writing (draft copy) revising, editing, and publishing.

INDIVIDUAL TITLE FOCUS & KEY CONCEPTS:
Fall 2007
This season will look at biography, poetry and two types of folktales—tall tales and myths. Previously, myths were cataloged with a Dewey number of 200 (religion) but have recently been reclassified to 398.2 (folktales.)

Poetry types of: (acrostic, limerick and couplet not included)
Free verse - lacks rhyme and has less predictable rhythm Example: Adoff, Arnold Black is Brown is Tan

Concrete poetry - words and phrases are arranged on paper to capture and extend the meaning. Each line should be a complete unit of thought. Looks like the thing itself.

Lyric poetry - written with rhythmic, song-like pattern, musical poetry

Diamonte

Haiku - Japanese form of poetry. Form is 17 syllables in three lines with pattern: first line, 5 syllables; second line 7 syllables; third line, 5 syllables. Usually has nature themes.

Cinquain - Syllabic verse form. Gradually increasing number of syllables in each line until the last line, which returns to two syllables.
Form for younger students:
...
TONE/APPROACH:
Tone should be accessible, energetic, and instructional. Must follow previously published formula. Individual titles must be unique while still fitting into the structure of the series.

(continued)
Show, not tell. Give examples and excerpts in addition to instruction the reader.

READER:

Grades: 4–6, ages 9–12
Reading Level: grade 5/6

SPECIFICATIONS
Language Arts

Trim Size: 6"x9"

Page Count: 64

Number of Chapters: 10

Getting Started
Setting the Scene
Characters
Viewpoint
Synopses and Plots
Winning Words
Scintillating Speech
Hints and Tips
The Next Step
Find Out More

Number of Spreads per Chapter: chapter length can vary with topic

FRONT MATTER:
Title page
CIP
Your Writing Journey
Table of Contents to include chapter and next level subheads

MAIN TEXT

Introduction must be genre relevant and include a definition of the genre. Main text must provide reader with a progression of tips and techniques that will show them to how to write an example of the specific genre, incorporating the characteristics of that genre.

FEATURES IN MAIN TEXT

(continued)
How to Use: gives reader an overview of the book
Writing assignment timeline: Includes chapter headings—gives reader visual of location in book
Tips and Techniques: Helpful hints to use and apply in writing journey
Now it's Your Turn: Includes an exercise or an activity to practice skill
Case Studies: Short synopsis about how a famous writer works, got their start, finds inspiration, etc.
Writers' Voices/ Quotes from books to demonstrate concept: Quotes used from popular children's books to illustrate concept discussed. For example, building suspense, creating dialogue, etc.

BACK MATTER

5 pages of back matter to include:

Glossary

On the Web
www.angelfire.com/wi/writingprocess
http://www.emints.org/ethemes/resources/S00000832.shtml

This on teaching biographies but may have other genre.
Young Authors' Workshop Resource Pages http://www.planet.eon.net/~bplaroch/

The Biography Maker www.bham.wednet.edu/bio/biomaker.htm
Biography Writer's Workshop with Patricia and Frederick McKissack
http://teacher.scholastic.com/writewit/biograph/

How to Write a Biography
http://www.infoplease.com/homework/wsbiography.html

How to Write an Interesting Biography
http://homeworktips.about.com/od/biography/a/bio.htm

Has lots of ads.
KidsWrite an e-zine for young authors and readers
www.kalwriters.com/kidswwrite

Myths

http://www.pantheon.org/areas/mythology/americas/native_american/articles.html

(continued)
http://www.bedtime-story.com/bedtime-story/indians.html

Poetry

Fern's Poetry Club http://pbskids.org/arthur/games/poetry/
(May be a little too primary.)
Magnificent Rainbow: Kids Form Poems
http://www.poetspath.com/exhibits/magnificentrainbow.html

Poetry Writing Workshop http://teacher.scholastic.com/writewit/poetry/index.htm

Cinquain – http://www.abcteach.com/Writing/cinquain.htm

Diamonte – http://www.abcteach.com/Writing/diamonte.htm

Haiku – http://www.abcteach.com/Contributions/HaikuInfo.htm

Free Verse http://falcon.jmu.edu/~ramseyil/poeform.htm

Read more historical fiction, tall tales, etc.
Booklist To include complete bibliographic information for the examples used in the text
Index
Photo Credits

ALIGNMENT WITH CURRICULUM STANDARDS:

National Council of Teachers of English and the International Reading Association

Students read a wide range of literature from many periods in many genres to build an understanding of the many dimensions

Students read a wide range of print and nonprint texts to build an understanding of texts, of themselves, and of the cultures of the United States and the world.

Students apply knowledge of language structure, language conventions (e.g., spelling and punctuation), media techniques, figurative language, and genre to create, critique, and discuss print and nonprint texts.

Students develop an understanding of and respect for diversity in language use, patterns, and dialects across cultures, ethnic groups, geographic regions, and social roles.

(continued)
Students use spoken, written, and visual language to accomplish their own purposes (e.g., for learning, enjoyment, persuasion, and the exchange of information).

Students employ a wide range of strategies as they write and use different writing process elements appropriately to communicate with different audiences for a variety of purposes.

Students use a variety of technological and information resources (e.g., libraries, databases, computer networks, video) to gather and synthesize information and to create and communicate knowledge.

OK, these aren't even the complete guidelines! I just wanted to give you *some* idea of the kind of guidance you will get from the publisher. The rest of the guidance will come from the other books in the series, and you'll want to closely examine those other books, as we talked about in the previous lesson.

Keep in mind that in the series guidelines, some information will be very useful, as when they say how many sentences should be in a spread, or when they point you to specific websites or books to use as central references.

Sometimes the guidelines will spell out things like, Chapter One will introduce the sport; Chapter Two will cover the history of the sport, etc. Or they might give you a spread-by-spread schedule, as in the first sample above (that's fairly rare, though!).

Meanwhile, other elements of the series guidelines will be totally useless to you. In the Write Your Own series guidelines, for instance, some of the info they provided was specific to titles in the series that I was not writing. So I could safely ignore all that info. I like to take a highlighter and highlight all the useful info in the guidelines. That helps me ignore the parts that don't really apply to me.

And please know that once you receive your series guidelines, they will make more sense as a whole than they do as excerpts. Your editor will be happy to answer any questions you have about the guidelines. And when you look at actual books in the series along **with** the guidelines, it will all make more sense!

HOMEWORK

No new homework. But you should finish up your writing sample(s) if you haven't already.

Lesson Fifteen

Readability Statistics

Readability statistics are numbers that tell you the reading level of a written passage. Theoretically, fourth graders would be able to read books at a 4th-grade readability. Or lower.

WHERE DO YOU FIND READABILITY STATISTICS?

In Microsoft Word 2010, click on File–Options–Proofing. Then look at the section that says "When correcting spelling and grammar in Word." Under that heading, click the box that says "Show readability statistics." When you have a passage or manuscript you want to check the readability of, click on Review–Spelling & Grammar. When the spell checking is complete, Word will show you readability statistics on your selection/manuscript. This is a box that shows how many words, how many paragraphs, average words per sentence, average letters per word, % of passive sentences, etc., and the Flesch-Kincaid reading grade level.

In Microsoft Word 2007, you can choose readability statistics by clicking Tools–Options–Spelling & Grammar, and then checking Show readability statistics. Then, when you have a passage or entire piece you want to check, you simply click on Tools–Spelling & Grammar. After it goes through and spell checks your work, it will show you a box that tells you how many words, how many paragraphs, average words per sentence, average letters per word, % of passive sentences, etc., and the Flesch-Kincaid reading grade level.

Keep in mind that the Word function that does this is not totally accurate in the sense that it doesn't come up with the same reading level that a reading specialist hand-evaluating your manuscript would come up with. But if you type in a sample that you're trying to match, it's really helpful.

HOW DO YOU USE THE READABILITY STATISTICS WHEN YOU'RE WRITING?

I use readability stats mostly in the revision process. Say the sample book the publisher gives me has 8.9 words per sentence and 3.2 characters per word, with a readability score of 4.2. But when I check my first draft, I come up with 12 words per sentence and 6.5 characters per word, with a readability score of 7.3. So I clearly need to get to a lower reading level. And two ways I can work on that are shortening my sentences and shortening my words.

For educational writing, where you're sometimes asked to write at a specific reading level, and where you're almost always asked to "match" sample books from the existing series, this can be a great revision tool.

CASE STUDY: REVISING WITH READABILITY STATS

For instance, when I was writing a book that was part of a craft series, I typed in the following sample from another book in the series, and Word gave me the Readability stats you'll see after the sample.

Beads Beyond Belief

Where do beads come from? Nearly everywhere! Beads can be found while you are on a walk in the woods, on the beach, or around your neighborhood. Keep a bag or container handy and be on the lookout for pebbles, seeds, and seashells with a small hole in them. Look around your house, too. Extra buttons make great beads. Garage sales and flea markets sell old jewelry that you can take apart and use in your own projects. Keep your eyes open and soon you will gather a large collection of things to string.

Craft stores carry beads in a variety of shapes, colors, and textures. Of course there are simple round beads, but there are more choices available. There is no limit to the silly, fun, and beautiful shapes you might find. Sparkling beads can add a lot of charm to any beaded creation.

You can also make your own beads. Most craft stores carry polymer clay that can be shaped into beads and then baked. Make sure to ask an adult for help. And don't forget to add the hole!

185 words
5.3 sentences per paragraph
11.3 words per sentence
4.2 characters per word
12% passive
79 reading ease
5.0 F-K

So as I was working on my own book for this series, I ran readability stats, chapter by chapter, on my first solid draft. When my F-K reading level was too high, I looked at the individual stats and figured out which component(s) I need to work on. For instance, if my characters per word number was 8.5, I was simply using too many long words. So I would go through and try to substitute shorter words when possible. Then I would rerun my readability stats to see if my F-K reading level had come closer to my target.

Many series have a range of readability. In that craft series, I think I typed in passages from three different books and ended up with F-K scores ranging from 4.8 to 6.1. That's common. The vocabulary associated with a topic may mean the readability is going to be higher, and you can't avoid that. But you should try to get as close as possible to the average of the samples you type in.

Please note: I know many writers for the educational market who do not use these stats in their writing. Some writers are more intuitive and just have an ear for what kind of writing matches what level of readability. So don't feel obligated to use this tool. I find it really useful, but you'll want to see what works best for you!

Lesson Sixteen

Working With an Editor

Perhaps you've already been published and have worked with editors. If so, some of this may be old hat for you. But working on assignment will be new to some of you, so I want to give you some tips on working with your editor.

Let me start with this. Almost every educational market editor I've worked with has been generous, patient, and kind. Almost every one has been appreciative of the hard work and effort I put into my manuscript. The editor is your business partner, and you both want to come out of the process feeling good about the whole project.

I'm proud to say I've done repeat writing for many publishers, and when I haven't, it's usually been my choice not to. I work hard to make a good impression on editors, to be a writer they'll want to work with again. Here are a couple of nice notes I've received:

Hi, Laura --

Well, you're batting .1000 this season, which is outstanding in this fickle league. Or any league for that matter.

Pardon the baseball metaphor. We would like to both of the stories you submitted the week ending Sept 29., "Graveyard of the Atlantic" and "Fire Goats."

As promised, we're paying $250 each for these two accepted works. Chris is out sick today, so with luck he'll mail the vouchers tomorrow.

Thank you for your contributions, your efforts, and your consideration. 80% of my work is dealing with pesky permissions departments at publishers and catering to their demands and procedures, so it's a treat for me to deal with people like yourself, personable, amenable and flexible.

If you have any questions, just ask.

Best,
Ben

Hi Laura,

These changes look fine, and I'll accept the manuscript today. Thanks!

Like the last batch of poetry books, I may have questions on edits or need minor adjustments once everything has been placed into layout. Also, I'll be sending pdfs and asking for comments once the books are pretty well put together. Despite all that, I probably won't be bugging you again until after the holidays, so enjoy the rest of the Christmas season! Thanks again for making this process fun, timely, and successful. :)

Happy holidays,

Jenny

Hi Laura,

I've attached the final, approved version of your pig poem. There were some very small changes, mostly to satisfy Literacy First's instructional needs. So I thought you might like to see the final version. Overall, though, this was one of the cleanest manuscripts I worked on for this series—so thanks for making our work easy! I especially appreciated that the rhyme scheme and meter was consistent to begin with.

Please understand that I'm sending this ms as a courtesy and not inviting further changes at this point. Also, some slight changes may still be made once pages are in layout (though the attached text should be very close to what is eventually printed).

All that said, if you notice that we've introduced something horrible, please let me know right away so I can fix it in page proofs.

Please also check that the byline name is as you want it.

Thanks again for the work on this! I hope we get to work together again soon.

Best,
Ben (different Ben from the first one)

OK, that's more than enough bragging on myself! I just want to show you that editors are nice, hardworking people. I have gotten more pats on the back as an educational writer than I ever did as a teacher (though that job, of course, had it its own rewards). They are so happy to work with writers who make their jobs easier!

So, how can you do that?

- Most importantly, follow directions. If an educational publisher hires you to write a 3,000-word straightforward informational book on volcanoes, don't turn in a 12,000-word epic that weaves volcano facts through a story of aliens landing on earth and observing virgin sacrifices to the volcano god. Give the editor what she asks for. This is especially crucial because your manuscript must match the others in the series!

- Follow the editor's lead in formality. Most will immediately be on a first name basis. But if you get emails to "Dear Ms. Wheeler, I am so pleased you'll be working with us," etc., you should respond in kind. "Dear Ms. Marks, I'm thrilled..." Let the editor set the tone for your correspondence.

- If you run into problems, check with the editor! Whether it's a content problem or a deadline problem, your best bet is to get the answer before you spend any more time. Think of yourself as a builder and the editor as the architect. The editor knows the overall vision of the finished book. You need to clearly understand that vision. The series' sample books will greatly help. But if it's a new series, you won't have samples. And either way, asking questions is fine. "I want to make sure I understand what you're looking for here. I thought I'd do XYZ. Does that sound like what you were expecting?"

- Be professional. Don't get emotional about dealing with the editor. You're both publishing professionals. (Yes, you are! Tell yourself that frequently if you need reminding and encouraging!) Be courteous and easy to work with, but not so enthusiastic you're bugging her 10 times a day with questions. I prefer email to phone calls, because then the editor can answer when she has time. I also like email because then I have a written record of the conversation. I tend to get flustered talking on the phone with editors, and my note-taking abilities suffer. But follow the editor's lead in this, of course. If she calls or wants to schedule a phone call, that's pretty much what you have to do. Also, even though most editors are very friendly, they are not there to hold your hand and offer constant reassurance! You shouldn't be emailing or calling constantly or you will be branded as a "high-maintenance writer." And editors who are shepherding anywhere from 20-50 books per season do not have time for high-maintenance writers. This is where having a critique group can be great, because you can run questions by them first. Then if nobody thinks the answer is clear, you email the editor.

- If you think you will have a problem meeting a deadline because of a home, work, or personal crisis, contact the editor **immediately**! Editors' biggest problem is writers not meeting deadlines. I have never missed a deadline and hope never to, but life happens, and I guess it's inevitable at some point! Soon, we'll talk a little about scheduling yourself and building in some extra time. But life still intervenes. The main thing is—never wait until the day before your book is due to say, "I actually don't even have the first draft done." Instead, as soon as you see a problem, talk with the editor. Once I asked an editor how set in stone a deadline was, because an illness was wreaking havoc with my schedule. The deadline was still weeks away, but the family illness put me behind. I thought I'd still make the deadline, but I wanted to touch base and find out if there was any give in the schedule. She assured me there was and gave me some extra time. I ended up being able to meet my original deadline, but I know the editor appreciated the heads-up.

OK, I don't want to sound like a Pollyanna. There have been a few editors I was glad to see the last of. Only a very small percentage, though. And even then, I tried to be ultra-courteous and professional in dealing with them. I tend to be a people-pleaser in my work life, but I've also learned to stand up for myself. Being assertive (but polite) is a sign of your competence and professionalism. It does not mean you are hard to deal with. Finding this balance can be a little tough, but with experience, you will get there (if you're not already).

HOMEWORK

Think about working with editors. What situations might come up that concern you? Now think about which people you might turn to to bounce questions/ideas off of. It's really helpful to have at least two or three writer friends you can turn to for advice. When you're wondering, "Should I ask the editor? Or is this clear to everyone but me?" ask those writer friends for their input. (This is also an area that Mentors for Rent is available to help with, as we do Q&A sessions with clients regarding the writing craft and the profession of writing. If you have access to professional writers who can help you, by all means, ask them! But if you have questions none of your friends/contacts can answer, feel free to ask Mentors for Rent for help.)

FAQ

1) *I'm nervous that I'll have tons of questions and the editor will think I'm too nit-picky.*

Remember, most editors are nit-picky when it comes to the editing stage (that's their job!), but very helpful and encouraging in the assigning and explaining stage.

An editor will know it's your first book (even though you don't *say* it in your cover letter, they will have figured that out from the omission). They will expect questions, and it's good to ask questions! Just group them so they're not overwhelming. And you could start your first email or phone call with, "As you know, this is my first book. I'm really excited, and I want to make sure I'm delivering what you want. Here are a few questions I have so far: x, y, z." Or something like that. They will really appreciate it. They'd rather you ask questions than turn in something way off the mark because you didn't really get it and tried to wing it.

On the other hand, if the guidelines and samples make it all incredibly clear, don't feel bad for having no questions. What you could do, about halfway to your deadline, is simply send off an email touching base with your editor and telling her that everything's going great with the book.

2) *What if I discover that I can't deliver what the editor wants?*

That's a great (and terrifying) question. First, don't be too hard on yourself. My first books for Capstone were for a brand new series. I had a hard time--they wanted so much info in so few words and I felt like a failure. But it turned out ALL their writers were having problems, even veterans. Capstone ended up TOTALLY revamping the books, making them much longer. They let us know what was going on, and some people probably had problems with some changes. I didn't. I was just glad they were going to be published, because for a while they were going to just scrap the whole series. Anyway, my experience is that if you are willing to do your best and to talk with the editor, 98% of the time, you can work things out.

Worst case scenario is that you truly **can't** deliver the book. That is **rare**. But if it happens, be honest with the editor. Be professional when you tell the editor (translation—don't cry!). Apologize kindly, and ask what you can do to mitigate the issues and delay you've caused. That might involve passing along your research to the replacement writer or something like that. Basically, do the best you can to make things right and to not burn your bridges. But again, this is a really rare thing! Don't go into your assignment thinking about failure. Have confidence in your research and writing abilities and dive into your book with enthusiasm!

3) *Do you ever use a pseudonym?*

Because the publisher owns your words, the editors can do what they want to them. Fears about what a book might end up as prompt some writers to consider using a pseudonym. But publishers, of course, want to put out accurate, attractive books. For me, the worst thing that has happened has been when "experts" or fact checkers brought in by the publishers introduce errors into the manuscript. If it's a topic you're truly an expert on, that can cause major problems. If I ever felt a book was coming out that contained errors, I would ask to use a pseudonym.

Also, sometimes you find a publisher is just doing a shoddy job of the project. Maybe it sounded good at first, but then you get the guidelines and they're a mess. Or the editor can't answer your questions, but you're under tight deadlines.

Any of those situations could result in a case where you might ask to have the book published under a different name. I have only done this a few times. On a couple of rhyming manuscripts recently that weren't quite my style. I'm more sensitive on rhyming manuscripts, because I love poetry and verse so much. So because there were a few things about the manuscripts that I really wasn't crazy about, I used a pen-name. I tried to be very tactful with my editor, of course. She seemed to understand—the changes that kept being made were not her choice—they were coming from someone who conceived the series but who wasn't really a writer or editor.

Related to these questions/fears about your assignment, here are a few warning signs to look for before you sign a contract:

- Being told that you'll have several contacts in the publishing company--that's always trouble, in my experience.
- An editor who can't really explain the project nor answer your questions.
- A brand new series with only vague guidelines.

If you run into any of these situations, it might not be the best project for you—especially for a first book!

Lesson Seventeen

Researching Your Book

Let's keep working on the skills you'll call on once you actually have an assignment. In the last lesson, we talked about working with editors, and today we'll discuss research.

Research is a basic skill that all nonfiction writers need, and it's a huge topic. Perhaps you're already an excellent researcher! In this lesson, I'm just going to share a bit of my process and technique, so that you can see how it goes. Perhaps you'll pick up a new resource or two.

WHERE DO YOU BEGIN?

First, I go to easybib.com and open a **new bibliography** for this book project. As I come across any reference I might possibly use, I enter it into easybib, and then when I need my sources cited list, easybib creates it for me. Easy! You can read more about why I love easybib in my blog entry:

http://laurasalas.wordpress.com/2009/08/25/tools-i-use-easybib-com-for-a-hassle-free-bibliography/
http://tinyurl.com/7cvnkwj

Next, I consider any **resources the publisher itself passes along** to me. For instance, when I wrote a couple of books about countries, my publisher let me know that the CIA World Factbook (online and easy to find/read) would be the baseline source for boundaries, population numbers, historical facts, etc. Of course, often, publishers don't pass along any resources! But if they do, I of course use those sources. I also check to see if they've given me any parameters for research. Some publishers will not allow writers to use any children's books for resources. Other publishers want three sources for every fact. Other publishers might have other particular directions for you.

I do **an Amazon search** to see what books, both children's and adults', have been published on my topic. I look for the most current books possible. Then I use this list to **choose books to put on reserve or interlibrary loan** at my own library.

When I have **books in hand, I read them to get a good overview** of the topic, and also to find more resources. Nonfiction books often have bibliographies or reading lists at the back. If I am having trouble finding information that I need, I might be able to **use these bibliographies or reading lists to find sources with more depth**.

But I actually **do most of my research online**. Most publishers don't have any problem with this, as long as I'm using reputable websites!

WHICH ONLINE RESOURCES CAN YOU USE?

Here are some characteristics of reputable websites:

- It might be produced and maintained by a recognized organization or entity, like the Smithsonian Institution, National Geographic, Museum of Modern Art, etc. Government websites also fall into this category. Well, not always. Some government websites are full of propaganda and unsupported statements. Generally, U.S. government sites are considered credible sources.

- It might be part of an educational institution. But be careful. Many universities provide web space for students, where students can put their research projects, etc. The info might be correct…or it might not. If the page isn't an ***official*** page of the institute, then it's not a credible source, even if it has the school's name in the url.

- It might be sponsored by a nonprofit group. But watch out for groups' agendas. When I wrote about snowmobiling, I double-checked stats from one non-profit group, because their agenda was to lobby for snowmobile access to national parks and other off-limits areas. So I had to make sure they weren't twisting facts to support their cause.

- It will tell you the credentials of the person or group that takes responsibility for the information on the site. Look for an About Me or About Us button to click on.

Basically, a personal webpage is not a good resource to use! Anybody can put *any* info on a website. It might be true or total fabrication! If a page seems well-done, professional, legitimate, then you can email the person whose page it is. Ask for their credentials and to use them as a source for your book.

One last online tool I frequently use is Lexis-Nexis: http://www.lexisnexis.com/. This is a pricey database of newspaper and magazine articles. Your library or local university might subscribe to it. Or your library might have access to other databases that will help you find up-to-the-minute articles on your topic. Basically, some online database that searches newspapers and magazines worldwide can be especially useful when you're writing about a science topic or anything current-event or issue-related. On some projects, I find I need to use lots of news articles for resources. On other projects, I never even need to use these at all.

WHAT ABOUT EXPERTS?

If you have a topic requiring you to research current developments in a specific field, or if you're writing a book for older readers, your depth of needed information will likely require you to interview some experts. One way to find experts is to find an organization online and then email them, explaining your search for an expert to answer questions and/or perhaps review your manuscript.

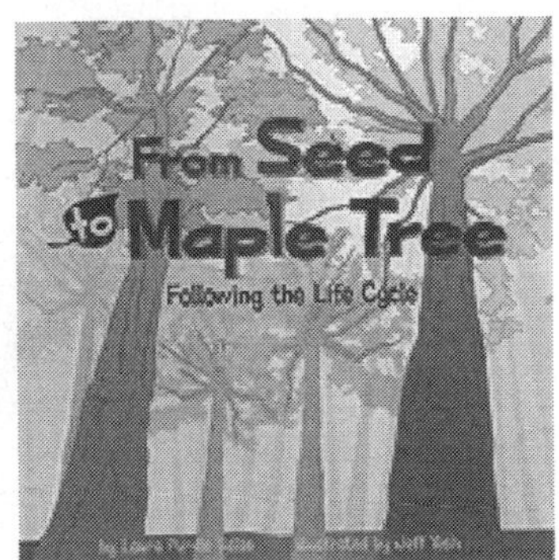

For instance, when I was writing about the life cycle of a maple tree, I wrote the following email after finding the Botanical Society of America online.

> Dear Botanical Society of America:
>
> I'm a children's writer with more than 30 nonfiction children's books published. My current assignment is a set of life-cycle books aimed at 1st-2nd graders. These books will be published by Picture Window Books (http://www.picturewindowbooks.com/) in 2008. One of the three titles I'm working on is Sugar Maple Tree.
>
> I'm a layperson, not a scientist, though I enjoy writing about scientific topics for children. I'm looking for an expert to read over my manuscript before I turn it in. I will be revising next week and am hoping to find a botanist who could read it the following week (Sep. 10-14). It's a very short book--less than 800 words, and it's due before the end of September.
>
> Do you know of a botanist who would be willing to read my manuscript and point out any errors to me?
>
> In addition, the publisher generally uses an expert adviser. I would pass along the name of whomever checks over my manuscript, and the publisher might choose to ask that person to officially read the manuscript (after the editing process). Then that person would be credited on the title page of the book.
>
> Please feel free to check out my website (www.laurasalas.com) for more information on my writing.
>
> Thanks for any help you can give me!
>
> Best,
> Laura Purdie Salas

Someone emailed me within a couple of days who was willing to help. I found similar experts for my other books in the series by emailing the University of Minnesota. I found its faculty list for the appropriate area (life sciences) and emailed the department heads for the areas that matched my other books.

But then I struggled finding experts on coral reefs and tundras. I found an organization, at least, to recommend for coral reefs. But tundras are not sexy, and there were fewer resources on that one. Not that there aren't experts out there. But finding them and corresponding with them—fast—was hard, especially in summer. I let the editor know of my troubles and left the expert-finding up to them.

In general, I have found people to be very generous with their time. I try to make it as easy as possible for them, of course.

WHEN RESEARCH FAILS?

So, in researching a book, I often use a mix of books, websites, articles, and real people (whom I almost always find online).

When I'm lost, which happens occasionally, I'll ask on the NFforKids list to see if anyone has any ideas for me. If I'm still batting.000, then I check at my local library. I also will ask a reference librarian at the Library of Congress' Ask a Librarian site.

http://www.loc.gov/rr/askalib/
http://tinyurl.com/14ev

They rock!

If I exhaust all my possibilities, then I will talk with the editor and explain the difficulties I'm having. At this point, it helps to have a list of everything you've tried, so that you still look as professional as possible!

SOME HELPFUL RESOURCES

If you're a beginning researcher, here are a few resources for you to explore at your leisure.

Research – Getting Started by Jan Fields
http://www.theinstituteofchildrensliterature.com/G2685/rx/wt06/getstarted.shtml
http://tinyurl.com/2dfobmh

Conducting Research from Purdue University
http://owl.english.purdue.edu/owl/section/2/8/
http://tinyurl.com/2exsgnl

Finding Information on the Internet from UC Berkeley
http://www.lib.berkeley.edu/TeachingLib/Guides/Internet/FindInfo.html
http://tinyurl.com/leqf

NCTE blog entry about **evaluating online resources**
http://ncteinbox.blogspot.com/2007/10/problem-with-pacific-northwest-tree.html
http://tinyurl.com/2mobkz

And here is a list of a few websites you might find handy if you're just learning to research online.

http://www.laurasalas.com/present/4_2_web.pdf
http://tinyurl.com/2clefpf

HOMEWORK

I would like you to imagine that you have been assigned a book for 4th–6th graders about how mountains are formed. Spend 30 minutes doing online research. Try to create a list of at least 15 resources you feel are reputable and that would be helpful to your work. You may list up to 6 books, but the rest should be websites or people you might contact for interviews or manuscript review. In your list, note where you found your people. Then evaluate how well you did. Don't feel bad if you weren't able to get 15 resources. The more you research, the faster you'll become!

FAQ

1) *Editors for magazines like* Highlights *are always saying they don't want encyclopedia research. The editors I've worked for in the education field seem happy to have encyclopedia research. Is that generally true for educational publishers?*

Interesting question about encyclopedias. Here's my impression. *Highlights* doesn't like encyclopedias because they don't want to see encyclopedic articles. In other words, many writers send in articles that are about "catfish" or "trees" or whatever. And that have simply summarized encyclopedia entries.

What they want are articles with focus/slant. Like "Battle of the Catfish: The struggle to save this big river fish" or "Knowing the Ropes: How daring scientists study rainforest trees." Something with a more specific angle that's engaging and requires much more research than simply encyclopedias.

So, I don't think the problem is with using an encyclopedia to START your research. It's just that it shouldn't END there.

My editors have been fine with my using encyclopedias as references. They only give me the most basic facts, but they're a good starting point sometimes.

2) *What about Wikipedia? I sometimes go there first because the entries often have a good overview and long lists of sources, but I never even put it on my bibliography because it's controversial. What do you think?*

I personally wouldn't ever list that on a resource list. There's too much uncited material there and it's not considered reputable (though its reputation is improving).

But, I do read Wikipedia entries and if the facts have citations, I then visit the source material and may decide to use it if it's both relevant and reputable. But I would then only put that source into my bib. I still wouldn't put the Wikipedia article itself in my bibliography.

3) *What if you can't find an expert through an organization?*

Sometimes researching newspaper articles on your topic will give you the names of experts in the field, and you can try contacting them.

Another useful source is Profnet (https://profnet.prnewswire.com/). Profnet is a network of experts (mostly university-affiliated professors/researchers) who are available for interviews. This is largely used by media folks to find experts to interview for stories, but if you have a fairly broad topic, you can use it to find an expert to talk with.

4) *Do you use primary sources?*

Primary sources (written BY the person actually involved in the topic/event) are ideal. But the amount of time you get to write your book (more on this soon) may be way too little to allow you to consult primary sources. I have very rarely used primary sources. Most educational publishers are fine with reputable secondary sources.

5) *Do you always turn in your bibliography? And do you have to put citations within your actual manuscript?*

This varies from publisher to publisher. And it can vary by how much you've written for a publisher and what level of trust they have in you. I always turn in a bibliography, but that's it, unless the publisher has specifically requested an annotated version of the manuscript.

I frequently keep track of my sources within the document using the Comment function in Word. At the end of each fact, I'll insert a Comment with the source info. I can show or hide those comments by clicking or unclicking a box, so I can show the publisher and print either with or without those comments.

Some publishers want an annotated version. Others (most of the ones I've dealt with) are content to know that if they ask you where you found a fact, you'll be able to quickly and easily provide them with your sources. But keep in mind that it's likely you WILL be asked at some point for the source of one of your facts. This is most common when the publisher's fact-checker can't quickly confirm the fact. So they'll ask for your source so that they can verify that your info is accurate.

Easybib also helps. As I enter each source, if it's a website (as many of my sources are), I click on "Add annotation." That opens a text box where I can actually just paste the info I've used from a specific site. This is most useful in books for younger kids. It could get unwieldy with books for the secondary audience.

Lesson Eighteen

Photo Research, Expert Consultants, Indices, and Permissions

In this lesson, we're going to talk about some of the other duties you might have besides writing the text of the book. There are a few other things that may or may not be part of your job as the writer. You should understand clearly from the contract (which we'll cover next) what your responsibilities are, and if you're unsure, ask the editor! Here are a few areas to think about.

PHOTO RESEARCH

Most editors would love to hear about great photos you come across in your research. Note the source (the book or the website or whatever) and send a list when you turn in your book. Editors will be very grateful for this, generally, since it makes the photo director's job much easier.

Some publishers actually require authors to obtain all photos out of their own money. Enslow is one of these, or at least they used to be. They generally don't pay any extra money for this, so the fees you will pay will come out of your advance. Negotiate for a bigger advance if this is the case! There are authors (but only a few that I know of) who actually like this, because it gives them more control over the book. They choose the images, they write the captions, and they know that the image is the right one to complement and extend the text.

Other writers, me included, hate this idea. It's extremely hard to estimate how much photos will cost, and I've heard writers talk about having to choose inferior photos just to stay within their budget. Enslow has great books, but some people think they're unappealing visually, and in large part this depends on the photos chosen.

Most educational publishers find the images themselves, and you will see the art when you get a copy of the manuscript to proofread (this is what's usually called galleys). At that point, if you see an error in a photo chosen or a caption, you can point it out.

So, always be clear on what your role is in the image-collection process! There's no right or wrong here. You just want to make sure you know what you have to do and that you're okay with whatever your responsibilities are.

EXPERT CONSULTANTS

Ask your editor! Some publishers require you to find an expert consultant to review your manuscript. Others handle it themselves but would just like suggestions from you. They're very grateful when you can recommend a source or two who was helpful to you! And the bonus is, if the expert consultant they use is the same one you found and who vetted your manuscript for you, then you know they already stand behind your book. For instance, in science topics, but also in other areas, you could have an expert review your manuscript. You make changes according to their comments, and then you turn it in. The publisher hires a different scientist to be the official expert consultant. That person has different opinions (scientists disagree about lots of things!). Then you end up revising again. And the person might even introduce errors into the manuscript, if they aren't a true expert and haven't done as much research as you (yes, that happens!). So it's great if you suggest an expert and the publisher ends up using him or her.

I have never paid an expert consultant. I am grateful and polite. I send a thank you note. I recommend them for the official consultant gig (at which point, they would be paid some stipend from the publisher).

Now, my books haven't been enormously long. If I had an expert consultant read a long manuscript, I'm not sure if they might bring up payment. Since I've always mentioned recommending them for the official expert gig, it hasn't come up. I think if in your request you mentioned that you would give them an acknowledgement, that would probably be much appreciated!

And as far as finding them, again, I usually turn to organizations and universities. They are ripe with generous people who want to make sure children are getting the most up-to-date information.

INDEXING

It's unusual that the writer is asked to create the index, but some publishers do have that policy. I just did one recently, and it wasn't bad. I kept a list of key words, and then I just alphabetized the list and searched for instances where it occurred in the book (using the Find function in Microsoft Word). This was a pretty short book, though. It would be tougher for a longer, more complex book. Really, indexing is kind of an art form, and hopefully your publishers will have an indexing service do it for them! But either way, you want to be clear on whether you have any part in the indexing process. This isn't something you want to be surprised with when you thought you were finished!

GETTING REPRINT PERMISSIONS

In the course of writing your book, you might use brief quotations by people. Fair use--the legal policy about how much of someone else's material you can use--is a complicated issue, but generally, when you're quoting one or two lines from something, it falls within fair use and you won't need to get permissions. But when you're quoting extensively or using crafts, recipes, poems, or songs from other people, you will need to get permission.

http://www.copyright.gov/fls/fl102.html
http://tinyurl.com/2ghlx

This is not an issue in 99% of educational market books. But I want to mention it because I ran into an issue with it once that caused quite a headache for all concerned.

I had accepted a book contract that involved using poems as examples, extensively. The editor gave me a list of suggested poetry collections to work from. I assumed that meant they had or could obtain permissions from those books. I wrote my book, using those sources. A while later, I got a frantic email from the editor saying she had forgotten all about permissions. Was it possible for me to take care of them?

No. It wasn't. Getting permissions from publishers is a **very** time-consuming thing. I had used 50+ poems in this book. Many were from anthologies (which usually don't even own the rights, so then you have to track down the original publication the poem was anthologized from). I probably would have spent more time getting these permissions than I did writing the book.

I don't say no to editors very often. I have gone above and beyond the call of duty to be helpful in almost every instance. But in this one, I had a little experience (thank goodness) in another project with getting reprint permissions and knew how time-consuming it was. So I replied with a polite email expressing concern and dismay that I was not able to do this. Long story short, they moved the publication date ahead to the next "publishing season" (most publishers have a spring and a fall line of books) and someone at the publisher took care of this task.

And I was offered another book by the editor, so I know I didn't burn my bridges.

We all want to write. We all want to be published. But in the course of being professional, remind yourself not to be a doormat!

All right, those are the main instances I can think of where your responsibilities might extend beyond writing text and sidebar or backmatter (fun facts, glossary, etc.) material.

One note: Photo research, index writing, etc., are topics that have been discussed thoroughly on the NFforKids list. If you join this list, and I hope you do, you can search the archives to read these discussions...and ask fresh questions, too!

HOMEWORK

If you haven't already, revise your writing sample(s). Try to get it in great shape so that it's ready to include in your introductory packets, which you should be sending out soon.

Get feedback on your writing sample! Here's what I'm looking for as I critique writing samples.

- Did the writer follow directions? In this case, I ask for one sample, up to 750 words long. A publisher might give you other specs. Whatever the directions are, editors are looking for writers who can follow very specific guidelines.
- Is the piece nonfiction?
- Is the piece for kids?

- Can I clearly tell whether the work is published or unpublished, edited or unedited?
- Has the writer identified what age range the piece is for?
- Has the writer identified the manuscript? For example, is it chapter one of a book? Is it a magazine article? The intro to a longer magazine article? Your writing sample should be clearly identified in the upper left corner!
- Is the manuscript professional–looking? Proper grammar, no typos, white paper, etc.?
- Is the writing clear and accurate?
- Does the tone and vocabulary of the writing generally match the age of the audience, as identified by the writer?

Those are the things I evaluate when I critique writing samples, and you might want to pass this list along to your own critique partners if they're the ones giving you feedback.

Lesson Nineteen

Assessment Writing

Many writers who write nonfiction books for the educational market also do some assessment writing. Assessment writing is not really part of my class or a big part of this workbook, but I thought some of you might be interested in some basic information. If you're not, please just skip this short chapter!

What is assessment writing? It is writing passages or items (questions) for standardized tests or for practice materials for those tests. As a parent and a lover of learning and reading, I am dismayed at the prevalence of standardized testing.

But I'll also admit that, as a student, I loved those things! The stories and poems and articles to read. The sharp pencils. The little bubbles to color in. Ah, good times!

And, as a writer and businessperson, I know this is one more income stream for me, and one more way to get my writing in front of kids. I have even had notes from teachers whose students loved my poems or stories in practice materials. How fun!

Loads of companies produce these materials. Some of these companies are tiny and pay very small fees. Others are bigger and pay larger fees.

I often make about $150 per passage, which could be a nonfiction passage, a short story, or a poem. Poetry and nonfiction are my standards. I've done a few stories, but find them to be more of a challenge. Other people are just the opposite, of course! Just depends on each writer's comfort zone.

Often in a passage, I am given specific standards that the passage must cover. In other words, if the questions for that passage will cover topic sentences or chronological structure, I have to make sure to write the passage (no matter what form it is) in a way that allows those kinds of questions to be asked. It's helpful to have some comfort level with what curriculum standards are in order to undertake these projects. I don't mean you have to have memorized them or anything, but knowledge of what standards are and what some of the current educational lingo is is enormously helpful. I have had to consult with teacher friends and do online research just to understand my directions from an editor at times!

Writing items or questions is even more demanding. The larger companies have many policies you have to adhere to regarding bias, unrealistic answers, referencing other questions…all sorts of things! I first started assessment writing with Riverside (the assessment branch of Houghton Mifflin), which flew a bunch of us to Chicago for training. I did regular work for them for several years, though then it just kind of came to a halt. But that training was really helpful for me!

Some assessment companies require that writers have degrees in certain content areas or have advanced degrees, but many do not.

So where do you find these assignments? Job boards are your best bet. First, check out the Writing for the Education Market blog (see the Resources list at the back of the book). Often, assessment-writing projects are listed there.

In addition to Monster.com and Craigslist.com (both of which I find clunky to use), here are some job boards that I check regularly when I'm beating the bushes for freelance work, which often includes assessment writing.

http://authorlink.monster.com/

http://www.writersweekly.com/

http://www.poewar.com/

http://www.sunoasis.com/freelance.html

http://www.freelancewriting.com/ (I like the Tuesday Morning Coffee newsletter)

http://www.journalismjobs.com/search_jobs_all.cfm

http://www.mediabistro.com/joblistings/Default.asp?gdsr=1&=0&jbdr=3

http://www.tjobs.com/index.php?cat=97

As you search the job boards, look for phrases like content writers, project writers, testing materials, etc. As with book contracts, I would not contract with an unknown company and do a lot of work without talking with other writers who have written for them.

Lesson Twenty

Fiction for Hire

OK, this topic is obviously outside the realm of a book titled *Writing Children's Nonfiction Books*... But every time, I taught this class, people asked about fiction, too, so I thought I'd briefly share what little info I know on this topic.

Yes, it is possible to write fiction for hire, though there are not tons of opportunities available.

One of the markets for fiction for hire is the assessment market. Assessment tests feature many short stories in the reading comprehension sections, and these are all flat-fee assignments. Assessment producers do sometimes buy reprint rights for magazine stories they like, but most of the reading comprehension stories are written on assignment for them.

I've only written a few stories for assessment materials. I started out by selling them stories I had already written (many of which I mistakenly thought were picture book manuscripts) and just hadn't been able to sell. I've also written a few specifically on assignment.

Check out Chapter Nineteen for resources for finding assessment assignments.

Another market for fiction for hire is educational publishers. A few of them do have fiction lines as well as nonfiction lines. As with nonfiction, these are series books. The publishers might have lines of fairy tale adaptations, or fictional stories highlighting certain social skills, or stories that utilize specific reading comprehension skills.

Again, some of these fiction projects integrate content material into the story (a story to illustrate a particular science concept, for instance), while others are just straight fiction stories.

I'm waiting right now to hear whether a fiction book of mine was accepted by an educational publisher who's doing a fiction series for reluctant readers. It's for 6th–graders, and I have my fingers crossed. It was tough for me to write! The editors were really helpful in giving me feedback and guidance. I wrote one other book for this series, and the editors accepted it. But the head people for the project rejected it. So, all I got was a small kill fee. I gave it one more shot and have my fingers crossed for this second book!

Your best bet for finding these assignments is to look at educational publishers' catalogs. Search the table of contents for fiction offerings and then check some of them out. If there's a line you're interested in, mention it in your introductory packet. If the publisher does both nonfiction and fiction, you could send writing samples in both areas.

In general, opportunities for writing fiction for hire can come about through job boards, contacts you make in the publishing industry, and approaching publishers directly. Good luck!

Lesson Twenty One

Money and Contracts

OK, you've been wondering about payment. There's a wide range of pay, and part of this career is finding books that you enjoy writing, and that you can write in a period of hours that makes them worth your time!

HOW MUCH WILL YOU GET PAID?

Here is a sampling of my fees for some of the books I've written:

- Isaac Newton biography for 4th–6th graders (Lerner): $3500
- Forest Fires for 3rd–4th graders (Capstone): $900
- Do Crocodiles Dance for K–1st graders (Picture Window Books): $900
- Scrapbooking for Fun for 4th graders (Compass Point): $1650

There is a direct correlation between length of book and pay. But it's also true that different publishers have different pay ranges. People on the NFforKids list are very open, typically, about sharing payment info, if you ask politely.

(You also get paid more if you write leveled readers. I don't recommend pursuing this kind of assignment until you do at least a few work-for-hire books first, so that you're comfortable with the general process. Here are a couple of pay examples from work-for-hire leveled readers:

The Thrill of the Ride: Skateboarding (high/low – 8th grade readers, 2nd grade reading level): $2800
Homelessness for 3rd grade readers: $2400

Leveled readers are a whole different ballgame and fairly complicated to write. You should be comfortable with readability, reading comprehension skills, etc. People with classroom teaching experience and educational writing experience are best suited for this. I wouldn't try it until you get some experience, though!)

KEEPING TRACK

To help me determine whether a project has been successful financially for me, I use slimtimer.com. This is a very cool little online tool. You create an account and then create tasks for your various writing projects. When you start working on a book, you open the site on your desktop and click that task. When you're done working on it for that day, you click off. Or if you change to a different project, take a break, eat lunch, whatever, you click on and off your projects, and it's an electronic time sheet. You can run reports and get how you spent all your time one week, month, year, etc. Or you can choose one project and see how much time you spent on it. Then you get little printable reports, like this.

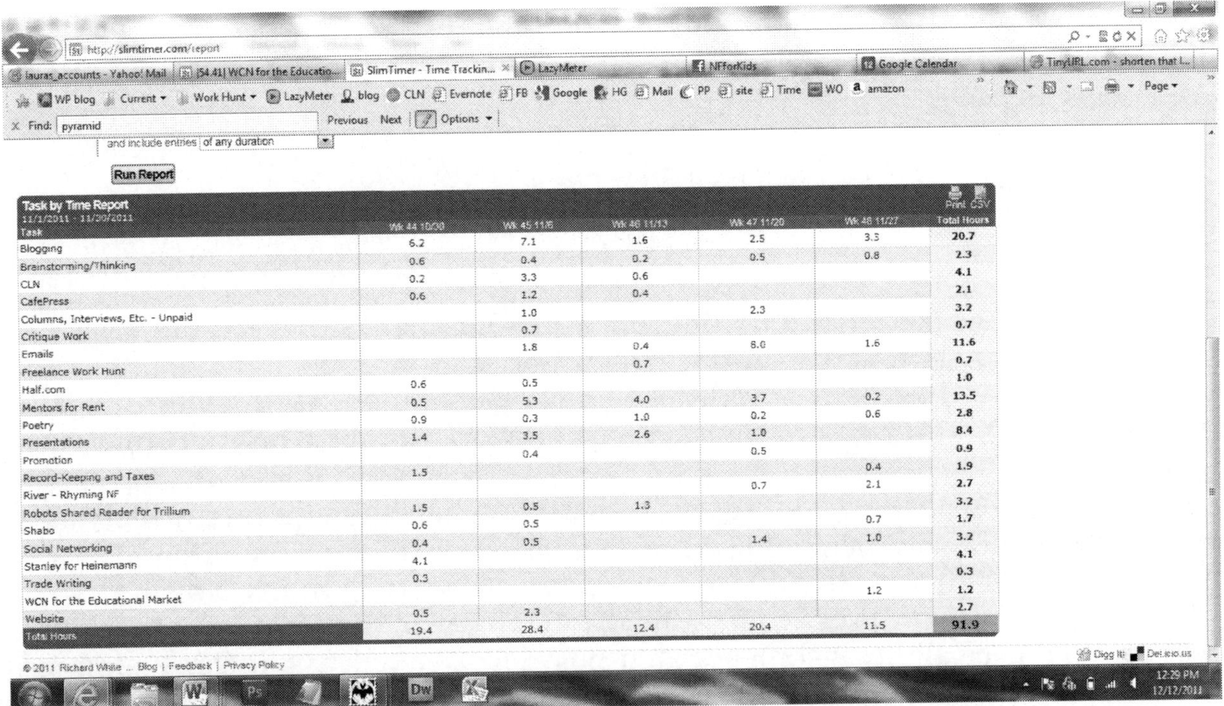

Task by Time Report
11/1/2011 - 11/30/2011

Task	Wk 44 10/30	Wk 45 11/6	Wk 46 11/13	Wk 47 11/20	Wk 48 11/27	Total Hours
Blogging	6.2	7.1	1.6	2.5	3.3	20.7
Brainstorming/Thinking	0.6	0.4	0.2	0.5	0.8	2.3
CLN	0.2	3.3	0.6			4.1
CafePress	0.6	1.2	0.4			2.1
Columns, Interviews, Etc. - Unpaid		1.0		2.3		3.2
Critique Work		0.7				0.7
Emails		1.8	0.4	8.0	1.6	11.6
Freelance Work Hunt			0.7			0.7
Half.com	0.6	0.5				1.0
Mentors for Rent	0.5	5.3	4.0	3.7	0.2	13.5
Poetry	0.9	0.3	1.0	0.2	0.6	2.8
Presentations	1.4	3.5	2.6	1.0		8.4
Promotion		0.4		0.5		0.9
Record-Keeping and Taxes	1.5				0.4	1.9
River - Rhyming NF				0.7	2.1	2.7
Robots Shared Reader for Trillium	1.5	0.5	1.3			3.2
Shabo	0.6	0.5			0.7	1.7
Social Networking	0.4	0.5		1.4	1.0	3.2
Stanley for Heinemann	4.1					4.1
Trade Writing	0.3					0.3
WCN for the Educational Market					1.2	1.2
Website	0.5	2.3				2.7
Total Hours	19.4	28.4	12.4	20.4	11.5	91.9

You can read more about how I use it here:

http://laurasalas.wordpress.com/2009/09/16/tools-i-use-clocking-in-with-slimtimer-com/
http://tinyurl.com/7lhpaze

So you get a chart with your projects down the left side, the months (or days or weeks, depending on what kind of report you run) across the top, and then totals at both sides. It's pretty cool.

When I'm done with a project, I look at a report of all my hours worked on that specific project, and then I take the fee and divide it by my total number of hours. That gives me my hourly rate for that project.

One summer, I wrote a set of 3 life-cycle books for Picture Window Books. The pay was $1,000 per book. I wrote the three books over the summer, and my time sheet shows that I worked a total of 19 hours. Now, I do forget to do my time sheet occasionally, or I might be thinking about the books while I'm out running errands or something. So this time probably does NOT represent 100% of the time I really spent on it. But even if I figure that I really spent perhaps 25 hours on the three books, that works out to $120 per hour. I love that! Many of my projects, unfortunately, don't come up to that kind of hourly pay! But when I look at various time sheets and pay amounts, it helps me see which topics, which age ranges, and which publishers tend to be the best fit for me, financially.

I also find that writing 3 or more books at a time for the same series tends to be more efficient. I group my research together, I only have to study one set of series guidelines, etc.

MAKING A LIVING

Obviously, you won't get rich writing work-for-hire books. But looking over my records for the past few years, I have made between $15,000 and $20,000 per year just on work-for-hire books. And that's only one component of my income, meaning I juggle several part-time "jobs," and work-for-hire books is one of them.

Each year for the past few years, I have shared my income info on my blog, as a way to share info with beginning writers or writers who are wondering if they can actually make a living at it. You can see my posts by going to my blog at http://laurasalas.wordpress.com/. Under Categories in the right sidebar, click on Money. You'll see all my income-related posts. To see only my income summaries, type in "How Much Money" in the Search box in the upper right corner of my blog.

I do know writers who support themselves full-time (obviously earning more than I do) doing this, usually supplementing with school visits. But it's definitely a freelance writing lifestyle, always hustling for jobs, etc. You'll have to figure out what you want to accomplish with it and set your goals accordingly. We'll talk about goals soon.

CONTRACTS

Work-for-hire contracts tend to be pretty simple and straightforward. But if you don't understand it, ask someone! Ask an attorney, or ask someone who's written for this company before. If you understand most of it but are unclear on one thing, just ask the editor or contract person for an explanation.

I don't use an attorney for my work-for-hire contracts. But if you want to have an attorney review your contract, here is one I can recommend.

Deb Orenstein - Her email address is mdkorenstein@mn.rr.com. I used her a couple of times and was very happy with her expertise.

Now, when you look at your contract, look for the basics: When is it due? How long is the manuscript? What do you get paid? When do you get paid? Can you buy copies at 50% off? Do you get free author copies? What rights are you selling?

You should get at least some of the money upon signing. If rest is due "upon acceptance," see if you can get some kind of a timeline in there: "within 4 weeks of receiving the final manuscript, publisher will notify author of acceptance. Balance of payment will be made within 4 weeks of that notification." Find out if you need to submit an invoice to be paid.

If you get no money on signing, try to talk to at least one other person who has written for this company and make sure it's a reputable publisher that does pay its writers!

Here's an example of a publisher's contract:

http://www.laurasalas.com/present/Contract.pdf
http://tinyurl.com/25fdtrd

They will all look a little bit different—each publisher has its own boilerplate contract. Read through this one, and see if it makes basic sense to you! And the contracts really haven't changed in the years I've been writing for the educational marketing. Some publishers have changed their payment schedules or their number of author copies provided, but basically, the terms remain pretty much the same.

CAN YOU NEGOTIATE FOR MORE MONEY?

Also, some of you may be wondering about negotiating contracts for better terms. In work-for-hire contracts, there's not a lot of room for negotiation. Especially when you're starting out. But as you write repeatedly for a publisher, or once you have more experience, you might be able to negotiate a higher fee.

I hate doing this because I'm not assertive about money issues, but I've gotten better (all part of being a professional writer, right?). So I will say, usually in an email, "Is $1200 the highest pay you can offer? Looking at the research and time involved, I was hoping to earn a higher fee than that." Or something along those lines, but in your own voice and personality.

With a Picture Window set of books I was writing, for instance, I negotiated the fee from $900 to $1000 per book, which is hardly anything. But it was $600 extra (for the series of books) for the simple effort of asking. On longer books with larger fees, I've negotiated increases of $2-500.

Another area that might be negotiable is author copies. I typically get 10 copies of each book I write, but I might be able to negotiate that upward if I wanted to.

HOMEWORK

1) Take stock of the progress you've made. Here's what I'd like you to have completed, ideally:

- Your list of three publishers to send your first packets to
- An editor's name for each of the publishers
- A copy of the submission guidelines for each, if available
- A basic cover letter template that you've had critiqued
- At least one children's nonfiction writing sample
- Business cards ordered
- Résumé, if applicable

2) If one or more of those items is incomplete, now is the time to buckle down and finish things up. If you have completed all of that—congratulations! You're doing an awesome job.

3) The next step is to customize your cover letter so that you have a personalized version for each of your three publishers. Make sure to personalize the name and address on each letter, as well as changing the specific info about that publisher's books and series that you like.

Lesson Twenty Two

Schedules and Goals

Now, I'd like to talk about how I schedule my time in working on a project. And I'd like you to set some goals for yourself.

SETTING A PROJECT SCHEDULE

Turn your manuscript in on time! That's what I've said is one of your absolutely top priorities! So how do you accomplish this? Well, you, of course, need to find the system that works best for you.

I'll share how I like to do it. First, I always try to factor in at least an extra week, if not two, into my schedule for emergencies (you know, those unexpected things that always happen at the worst possible times).

I like to look at the calendar and work backward from my book's due date. Using a real-life example, on January 18 I received the guidelines for a science songs project that I had accepted. The books, four of them, were due on April 1. In most cases, I would already have started gathering research materials as soon as I knew the topic of the book, and I would already have some of those in hand by the time I got the guidelines. But this time, I didn't even know the topics until I received the guidelines. So I was starting from absolute scratch here.

OK, my deadline was April 1. I wanted to build in that extra time for emergencies. So I set my personal deadline for this project as March 21. That was about a week and a half early, and it was also the beginning of spring break for my kids. So if I was able to finish the project by then, it would work really nicely for my schedule and would also be a bonus for the editor I was working with. If something happened like an illness or unexpected travel or something, I had that padding of a week and a half to allow for it.

If I wanted to be able to turn them in on March 21, I wanted a pretty good draft done by March 7. That gave me two full weeks to polish. Because this was four books, and they were rhyming books in a set meter, I needed that much time. Often, I would only use one week for polishing time.

In order to have a pretty good draft by March 7, I needed my first draft done by February 22. That gave me two weeks to work on getting more facts into the songs and finishing up any last-minute research I needed to do. That's probably the time during which I would write my sidebars and end matter.

To have the first draft done by February 22, I wanted to have my research done by February 1. That gave me 3 weeks to turn my collection of facts into rough songs.

February 1 was two weeks from January 18, which meant I had that much time to do my basic research. I had to get going!

That works out about right, actually. I typically (though it varies) devote about 25% of my time to research. From January 18 until March 21 is actually 10 weeks, but two weeks of research feels right. The form of these books would be more complicated than my usual projects, so I wanted to get that research done and get started on the writing.

However, even once my basic research was done (by February 1), I would no doubt have some lingering questions that I was still trying to find answers to. The goal was for the bulk of my research to be completed by then. I wanted to have learned enough that I had synthesized the info in my brain and felt ready to sit down and start writing.

And it worked out well. I followed my plan (juggling my other teaching, working, and writing duties with an hour or two of time on these books each day). I turned in my manuscripts on March 14, and the editor was thrilled to have them so early. I had a bit more revision time on these than usual, because my straight nonfiction books, for a publisher I've worked with before, often now don't need much revision (though that wasn't true for the first many books I wrote). But with this rhyming verse, if they didn't like a line, it changed many other lines.

But, once the books were at the printer, I ran my slimtimer report on this project. I see I logged about 23 hours of butt-in-chair time on this project. And the pay was

$4,000. So these worked out really well for me ($174 per hour) and I enjoyed them! This particular project was a really good match for me. It will be up to you to learn (through thinking about it and through trial and error) which projects are good matches for you. It will likely be very different kinds of projects than the ones that work best for me. And that's a good thing! There are such a wide variety of kinds of projects available. Your educational writing will become much more rewarding and fun once you try some different things and discover where your niche is.

YOUR EDUCATIONAL WRITING GOALS

Now, it's time for YOU to set some goals.

Here are the goals I laid out for you at the beginning of this workbook:

- understand the difference between writing for the trade and educational markets
- know whether writing books for the educational market is likely to be a good fit for you
- understand how to approach publishers for writing assignments
- have a good start on all the components you need for your introductory packets
- have identified at least 3 publishers to approach
- have a self-imposed deadline for sending out those 3 introductory packets (if you haven't already sent some or all of them right now)
- feel confident about your researching and writing skills, as well as your techniques for working with an editor

What do you think? Has this workbook enabled you to meet these goals? Are you ready to send out your introductory packets and start pursuing work in the educational market? I hope so!

HOMEWORK

What I would like you to do is write a short statement about what the next step is for you. Where do you want to go from here? What is your due date for doing it?

Your next step might be mailing 1 intro packet by the end of this month. Or it might be more intense. Maybe you hope to get 5 packets out next week. Or maybe you plan to work over spring break or winter break or summer, if you're an educator. Your goals should push you farther than you've gone, but they should be realistic, too. We all have different lives. Some work full-time outside of the home, while some are devoting all our time to writing. Some have small children or aging parents to care for. Some are doing many kinds of writing. Some aren't. Please do **NOT** feel like your goal isn't worthy if it doesn't sound big. This goal is just for **you**!

And next, start working toward that goal! Ideally, I hope you have your three first packets ready to mail out. But if not, that's fine. Just set a goal that is realistic but forces you to stretch a little bit!

I wish you the very best of luck in breaking into this market. There is enough work here for many, many writers. If you do your best work and you are persistent (this is KEY), you *can* do it! I hope you'll let me know of your successes when you have them.

ADDITIONAL RESOURCES

Resources for Nonfiction Writers

http://groups.yahoo.com/group/NFforKids/ -- a Yahoo list just for kids' nonfiction writers. Full of helpful, knowledgeable writers, great for newbies and more experienced writers.

http://www.underdown.org/index.html -- website maintained by writer/editor Harold Underdown

http://www.fionabayrock.com/ -- website maintained by writer Fiona Bayrock

http://www.institutechildrenslit.com/rx/wt06/index.shtml -- Articles on writing nonfiction from the Institute of Children's Literature

http://www.evelynchristensen.com/markets.html - Evelyn B. Christensen - list of educational publishers

http://educationwriting.blogspot.com/ - Blog - Writing for the Education Market - regular leads for educational writers. An excellent resource!

http://www.writersdigest.com/writing-articles/by-writing-genre/nonfiction-by-writing-genre - *Writer's Digest* articles about nonfiction (not children's-writing specific)

Your library's children's librarian

Society of Children's Book Writers & Illustrators - http://www.scbwi.org/ or SCBWI, 8271 Beverly Blvd., Los Angeles, CA 90048. 323-782-1010

Children's Literature Network - http://www.childrensliteraturenetwork.org/index.php or Children's Literature Network, PO Box 46163, Plymouth, MN 55446-0163

http://www.renlearn.com/store/quiz_home.asp - Renaissance Learning. You can put in almost any book title and get the exact word count, the reading level, etc.

http://blog.nathanbransford.com/2007/02/how-to-write-nonfiction-book-proposal.html -- "How to Write a Book Proposal," by author and former literary agent Nathan Bransford

http://laurasalas.wordpress.com/ -- My blog

http://www.vistaprint.com/ - Inexpensive business cards, promo postcards, etc.

http://www.slimtimer.com/ – Nifty online time sheet system

http://www.easybib.com – A wonderful free online bibliography service!

Newsletters: Children's Writer: http://www.childrenswriter.com/

Children's Book Insider: http://www.write4kids.com/aboutcbi.html

Yes! You Can Learn How to Write Children's Books, Get Them Published, and Build a Successful Writing Career: Excellent book for those wanting to build a true career. By Nancy I. Sanders.

http://www.amazon.com/Childrens-Published-Successful-Writing-Career/dp/0979160669/ref=sr_1_1?ie=UTF8&s=books&qid=1273851849&sr=8-1
http://tinyurl.com/2dh7jht

Catalog Analysis Form

Publisher:

Date of catalog:

Age range:

Subject areas:

One-author series?

Is the look of the books appealing, in general?

Any award-winning books?

Which age range appeals to you most for this publisher?

3 series (multi-author) that appeal to me (length, style, topics, etc.):

1.

2.

3.

Overall impression:

Publisher Analysis Form

Publisher: Date:

<u>The Books</u>

Imprints/lines:

Age range and word counts:

1)

2)

3)

Subject areas:

High/lows? If so, ages/grade levels/word counts:

Series only?

Style of art (photos, illustrations, color, b/w?):

One-author series?

Imprints or lines I'm interested in:

Particular series that appeal to me:

1)

2)

3)

Making Contact

Guidelines available?

How to contact:

Any personal contact with an editor?

Writing for this Company

Work-for-hire or royalty/advance?

Typical pay:

Payment schedule:

All rights?

Author responsible for art?

Author indexes?

Typical turnaround time?

Who else has written for this company?

1)

2)

3)

Series Analysis Form

Publisher: Series:

Age range:

Title	Wds	Pgs	Chs	Lead	POV	Tone	Extras	Misc

Made in the USA
San Bernardino, CA
20 April 2016